A
WRINKLIES™
TRIP DOWN MEMORY LANE

First published in Great Britain in 2013 by Prion Books

an imprint of the
Carlton Publishing Group
20 Mortimer Street
London W1T 3JW

The material in this book was previously published
in *The Wrinklies' Reminiscellany* in 2011.

Text copyright © 2013 Mike Haskins and Clive Whichelow
Layout and design copyright © 2013 Carlton Books Ltd

A catalogue record for this book is available from the British Library

ISBN 978-1-85375-900-0

Printed in Great Britain by CPI Group (UK) Ltd, Croydon, CR0 4YY

10 9 8 7 6 5 4 3 2 1

A
WRINKLIES™
TRIP DOWN MEMORY LANE

A miscellany of the good old days

Mike Haskins
& Clive Whichelow

PRION

Introduction

Do you sometimes feel that things aren't what they used to be?

The only problem is that with your memory being what it is these days you can't be too sure.

You can just about remember proper money – pounds, shillings and pence and of course, tanners, bobs and threepenny bits – but can you remember what they looked like? Didn't halfpennies have little ships on them – or was that farthings? You see, it's all getting lost in the mists of time or, more to the point, the mists of your increasingly dodgy memory.

Then there were the sweets. Jamboree Bags, for example; sweet cigarettes, Five Boys chocolate... ah, yes, it's all coming back now, isn't it?

And that, my friend, is the whole point of this book. It's a sort of miscellany of reminiscences – a *Reminiscellany*, if you will. Leafing through its pages you will find your past life flashing before you – but not in an "Oh, my giddy aunt", near-death-experience sort of way: more of an "Ah, those were the good old days" sort of way.

Can't remember the names of the Goons characters or their catchphrases? You silly, twisted boy – just flick through your trusty *Reminiscellany*! Can't remember the name of those cigarettes you used to smoke in the days before they were bad for you? From Anchor to Woodbine, you'll probably find them here.

Do you remember when there seemed to be a western on TV every night of the week? Of course you do: but which one was it that had Chester saying "All right, Mr Dillon?" Was it *Rawhide*, *Gunsmoke* or *Wagon Train*?

Introduction

You may also be old enough to remember food rationing, but what exactly were those allowances? Was it two ounces of butter and four of margarine – or was it the other way round? All shall be revealed!

And those Churchill speeches – was it "Blood, sweat and tears", or was that a 1960s jazz-rock band? And what exactly was it that Chamberlain said in September 1939? You can remember the bit about "No such understanding has been received", but what was the rest of it?

Then there were the drinks – Double Diamond, Skol lager, Watney's Red Barrel, Bols advocaat... whatever happened to them all?

And the magazines and newspapers: *Titbits*, *Reveille*, *The Daily Sketch*, *Practical Mechanics*... and the comics! *The Beezer*, for example – was that the one with Colonel Blink, or was he in the *Topper*?

You may also be old enough to remember trying to form a skiffle band, but what were the essential ingredients?

Apart from all those things you've forgotten, there are all those things they keep changing: names of places, for example. Now, what was it that Beijing used to be called? or Iran? or Mumbai? – and whatever happened to the West Riding of Yorkshire? Sold off to some foreign conglomerate, no doubt.

But you no longer need to rack those addled, wrinkly brains, because all this handy info is herein contained.

Whacko!

Mike Haskins & Clive Whichelow

Countries that are no longer part of the British Empire

Year gained independence		Formerly known as
1901	Australia	
1910	South Africa	
1922	Ireland	
1922	Egypt	
1926	Canada	
1932	Iraq	
1947	New Zealand	
1947	India	India (part of)
1947	Pakistan	India (part of)
1948	Israel	Palestine
1948	Jordan	Transjordan
1948	Myanmar	Burma
1948	Sri Lanka	Ceylon
1949	Canada (part of)	Newfoundland
1954	Sudan	
1957	Ghana	Gold Coast
1960	Cyprus	
1960	Nigeria	
1960	Somaliland	British Somaliland
1961	Kuwait	
1961	Mauritius	
1961	Sierra Leone	
1961	Cameroon	British Cameroon
1962	Uganda	
1962	Western Samoa	
1962	Trinidad & Tobago	Trinidad
1963	Jamaica	
1963	Kenya	
1963	Singapore	
1963	Malawi	Nyasaland
1963	Tanzania (part of)	Tanganyika

Year gained independence		Formerly known as
1963	Tanzania (part of)	Zanzibar
1964	Malta	
1964	Zambia (part of)	Rhodesia
1965	Gambia	
1965	East Malaysia	Sarawak
1965	Sabah	North Borneo
1965	West Malaysia	Malaya
1966	Barbados	
1966	Botswana	Bechuanaland
1966	Guyana	British Guyana
1966	Lesotho	Basutoland
1967	Yemen	Aden
1968	Swaziland	
1970	Fiji	
1970	Tonga	
1971	Bahrain	
1971	United Arab Emirates	Trucial Oman
1973	Bahamas	
1974	Grenada	
1976	Maldive Islands	
1976	Papua New Guinea	
1976	Seychelles	
1978	Solomon Islands	British Solomon Islands
1979	St Lucia	
1979	St Vincent	
1979	Kiribati & Tuvalu	Gilbert & Ellice Islands
1979	Zimbabwe (part of)	Rhodesia
1980	Vanuatu	New Hebrides
1981	Belize	British Honduras
1983	St Kitts/Nevis	St Kitts
1984	Brunei	
1997	Hong Kong	

The British Empire today

• Montserrat • Cayman Islands • Channel Islands
Pitcairn Island • Cook Islands • Ascension Island • St Helena
Falkland Islands • Anguilla • Tristan Da Cunha • Gibraltar
Bermuda • Turks and Caicos Islands

Historic British Banknotes

The ten-shilling note

First issued by the Bank of England:	November 22, 1928
Colour of note:	Predominantly red-brown
Illustration:	Britannia
Colour during WW2:	Mauve
Portrait of Queen added to design:	October 12, 1961
Withdrawn from circulation:	November 20, 1970
Replaced by:	50p coin (issued from October 1969)

The one-pound note

First issued by the Bank of England:	1797-1845
Reintroduced:	November 22, 1928
Colour of note:	Predominantly green
Illustration:	Britannia
Colour during WW2:	Pink
Portrait of Queen added to design:	March 17, 1960
Withdrawn from circulation:	May 31, 1979
Replaced by:	Pictorial series of notes

The five-pound note

First issued by the Bank of England:	1793-March 13, 1961
Colour of note:	White ("The White Fiver")
Illustration:	None: black lettering on white paper
Replacement note issued:	February 21, 1957
Colour of note:	Dark blue
Illustration:	Britannia
Portrait of Queen added to design:	February 21, 1963
Withdrawn from circulation:	August 31, 1973
Replaced by:	Pictorial series of notes

The ten-pound note

First issued by the Bank of England:	1759-April 16, 1945
Reintroduced:	February 21, 1964
Colour of note:	Brown
Illustration:	Queen Elizabeth II
Withdrawn from circulation:	May 31, 1979
Replaced by:	Pictorial series of notes

Inventions from 1900-1948

- 1900 The escalator;
  the Zeppelin.
- 1901 The vacuum cleaner;
  the double-edged
  safety razor.
- 1902 The air conditioner;
  neon light;
  the teddy bear.
- 1903 The aeroplane;
  windscreen wipers.
- 1904 Teabags;
  the tractor.
- 1906 Corn flakes.
- 1907 Bakelite *(the first
  synthetic plastic)*;
  colour photography;
  the helicopter.
- 1908 Cellophane;
  the Geiger counter.
- 1909 Instant coffee.

- 1910 Talking motion pictures.
- 1912 The tank.
- 1913 The crossword puzzle;
  the bra;
  the zip.
- 1914 The gas mask.
- 1915 Pyrex.
- 1916 Stainless steel.
- 1919 The pop-up toaster;
  flip-flops.

- 1920 Band-Aid plasters.
- 1921 The lie detector.
- 1923 Traffic signals;
  frozen food;
  the cathode-ray tube.
- 1924 The spiral-bound
  notebook.
- 1925 Mechanical television.

- 1926 Liquid-fuelled rockets.
- 1927 The quartz watch;
  Technicolor;
  electronic television.
- 1928 Penicillin;
  the electric shaver;
  bubble gum.
- 1929 The car radio.

- 1930 The jet engine;
  Scotch sticky tape;
  the analogue computer.
- 1932 The radio telescope;
  Polaroid photography;
  the zoom lens;
  the parking meter.
- 1933 FM radio;
  stereophonic recording.
- 1934 Cat's eyes;
  the tape recorder.
- 1935 Radar;
  nylon;
  canned beer.
- 1937 The photocopier.
- 1938 The ballpoint pen;
  LSD;
  Teflon.

- 1940 Colour television.
- 1941 The aerosol spray can.
- 1942 The electronic digital
  computer.
- 1943 The Slinky.
- 1945 The atomic bomb.
- 1946 The microwave oven.
- 1947 The mobile phone;
  Tupperware.
- 1948 The Frisbee®;
  Velcro®;
  the jukebox.

Most popular names given to children born in England and Wales during the 20th century

BOYS

	1904	1924	1944	1954	1964	1974
1	William	John	John	David	David	Paul
2	John	William	David	John	Paul	Mark
3	George	George	Michael	Stephen	Andrew	David
4	Thomas	James	Peter	Michael	Mark	Andrew
5	Arthur	Thomas	Robert	Peter	John	Richard
6	James	Ronald	Anthony	Robert	Michael	Christopher
7	Charles	Kenneth	Brian	Paul	Stephen	James
8	Frederick	Robert	Alan	Alan	Ian	Simon
9	Albert	Arthur	William	Christopher	Robert	Michael
10	Ernest	Frederick	James	Richard	Richard	Matthew

GIRLS

	1904	1924	1944	1954	1964	1974
1	Mary	Margaret	Margaret	Susan	Susan	Sarah
2	Florence	Mary	Patricia	Linda	Julie	Claire
3	Doris	Joan	Christine	Christine	Karen	Nicola
4	Edith	Joyce	Mary	Margaret	Jacqueline	Emma
5	Dorothy	Dorothy	Jean	Janet	Deborah	Lisa
6	Annie	Kathleen	Ann	Patricia	Tracey	Joanne
7	Margaret	Doris	Susan	Carol	Jane	Michelle
8	Alice	Irene	Janet	Elizabeth	Helen	Helen
9	Elizabeth	Elizabeth	Maureen	Mary	Diane	Samantha
10	Elsie	Eileen	Barbara	Anne	Sharon	Karen

Census estimates of UK population over the past century

1901	1911	1921	1931	1951
38,237,000	42,082,000	44,027,000	46,038,000	50,225,000

1961	1971	1981	1991	2001
52,807,000	55,928,000	56,357,000	57,439,000	59,113,000

Annual budget

As suggested in *Good Housekeeping* magazine in 1931 for a family living on an income of £410 a year.

Income tax	Nil
Rent, property tax, rates	£80
Household expenses including food, wages, laundry, light and fuel	£152
Education	£30
Clothing, personal allowances and charity	£66
Holidays, amusements or upkeep of car	£30
Insurance saving	£35
Incidental expenses including doctor and dentist etc	£17
Total	**£410**

Acronyms used on love letters

SWALK	Sealed with a loving kiss.
BURMA	Be upstairs ready my angel. *or* Be undressed and ready, my angel.
BOLTOP	Better on lips than on paper.
HOLLAND	Hope our love lasts and never dies.
ITALY	I trust and love you.
WALES	With a love eternal, sweetheart.
MEXICO CITY	May every kiss (x) I can offer carry itself to you.
MALAYA	My ardent lips await your arrival.
BELFAST	Be ever loving, faithful and stay true.
CHINA	Come home, I need affection.
TSTSTSA	To someone too sweet to sleep alone.
SWPAP	Sprinkled with perfume and powder.

And of course…

NORWICH	Knickers off ready when I come home (as Alan Bennett once said, "Yes, I know 'knickers' is spelt with a 'k'!").

Imperial measurements of length

1 league = 3 miles, based on the distance a man could walk in 1 hour.

1 mile = 1,760 yards (1.6 kilometres). Originally the Roman mile was 5,000 feet but this was extended to 5,280 to make a mile exactly 8 furlongs.

1 furlong = ¹/₈ mile or 220 yards (201.17 metres), from the Old English "furh lang" or "furrow long", based on the length of a single plough's furrow in a medieval open field.

1 chain = 22 yards or ¹/₁₀ furlong (20.12 metres), the length of a surveyor's chain.

1 pole = 5 ½ yards or ¼ chain (5.03 metres); the pole was a long stick used to control teams of oxen in the fields.

1 rod = An alternative name for the pole.

1 perch = Another alternative name for the pole.

1 fathom = 2 yards (1.8288 metres), traditionally used for measuring the depth of water.

1 yard = 3 feet or 36 inches (0.9144 metres), from the word for a straight branch or rod.

1 foot = 12 inches (0.3048 metres).

1 link = Just under 8 inches (20.12 centimetres); there were a hundred links in the surveyor's chain!

1 inch = ¹/₁₂ foot, from the Latin "uncia" meaning a twelfth part, which also gave us the word "ounce".

Older measurements of length

1 cubit = 18 inches or ½ yard.

1 span = 9 inches, the distance across the outstretched hand from the tip of the thumb to the tip of the little finger.

1 shaftment = 6 inches, the distance across the outstretched hand from the tip of the thumb to the other side of the fist.

1 hand = 4 inches, the width of the palm including the non-outstretched thumb; still used in the measurement of horses.

1 barleycorn = ¹/₃ inch, the length of a corn of barley.

1 poppyseed = ¼ barleycorn.
or **1 line**

How much was money worth?

The table below shows the spending value of £1 in years gone by in today's money (calculated with regard to average earnings at the time).

1900	1920	1930	1940	1950	1960	1970	1980
£436	£136	£193	£139	£75.90	£39.70	£20.90	£4.97

The table below shows the amount of money in years gone by that would be equivalent to £100 in today's money (again calculated with regard to average earnings at the time).

1900	1920	1930	1940	1950	1960	1970	1980
4s 7d	14s 9d	10s 5d	£1 6s 5d	£1 6s 5d	£2 10s 5d	£4 15s 7d	£20.10

Britain's first postage stamps

Penny black: The world's first adhesive postage stamp, issued in the UK in 1840.

Twopenny blue: The second British stamp after the penny black.

Penny red: The successor to the penny black, issued in 1841.

The school day as we knew it: the school bell

- The school bell was a proper handbell, not some electronic device.
- It was rung by a teacher or a monitor.
- As in a pub, there was a "first bell" and a "second bell".
- If you came in after the second bell you were marked as late.

Rowntree's

Rowntree's was founded in York in 1862 by Henry Rowntree, whose brother Joseph joined him in the business seven years later. Among their products were:

Fruit Pastilles etc: Fruit Pastilles were first made by Rowntree's in Fawdon, Tyneside, in 1881. Prior to this, gums and pastilles had only been produced in France. Rowntree's Fruit Gums were introduced in 1893.

Smarties: Rowntree's marketed Chocolate Beans from 1882. Name changed to Smarties Chocolate Beans in 1937. During the war, Smarties were 9 ½ d for a ¼ lb.

Black Magic: Launched in 1933. A ¼ lb box cost 9d, a 1lb box 2s 10d.

Kit Kat: Launched August 1935 as Rowntree's Chocolate Crisp (price 2d). Renamed in 1937 as Kit Kat Chocolate Crisp. Packaging was originally red but switched to blue during WW2 before reverting to red.

Aero: Launched in the north of England in 1935 as "the new chocolate" (price 2d) before quickly going nationwide. Unavailable for nine years because of wartime milk shortages. Relaunched 1950.

Dairy Box: Launched 1936 as Dairy Assortment. A ½ lb box cost 1s. In the 1930s, the chocolates as detailed on a tin of Dairy Box were: Turkish Delight/ Burnt Almond Toffee/ Wafer Biscuit Sandwich/ Aero/ Almond Crispy Cluster/ Coffee Crème/ Hazelnut Log/ Nougat de Montelimar/ Cracknel and Praline Sandwich.

Yorkie Launched in 1976 by what was then Rowntree Mackintosh as a chunkier rival to Cadbury's Dairy Milk.

Rowntree's also launched Blue Riband (1936), Polo Mints (1948), Polo Fruits (1953), After Eight (1962), Tooty Frooties (1963), Jelly Tots (1967) and Matchmakers (1969).

The announcement of war

This morning the British Ambassador in Berlin handed the German
Government a final note stating that, unless we heard from them by eleven
o'clock that they were prepared at once to withdraw their troops from Poland,
a state of war would exist between us.
I have to tell you that no such undertaking has been received, and that
consequently this country is at war with Germany.

Neville Chamberlain, September 3, 1939

Army and Air Force slang

Axle grease – butter
Beer boy – inexperienced flier
Big Bertha – German gun
Bint – young lady
Bivvy – bivouac
or makeshift camp
Blighty – England
Blimp – non-rigid airship
Buckshee – free of charge
Bully beef – tinned beef
Bumf – toilet paper *or*
excessive paperwork
Canteen medals – stains on uniform
Chit – receipt or note
Conchie – conscientious
objector
Dekko – look, as in "take a
dekko"

Doggo – hiding
Doolally – mad
Flak – anti-aircraft fire
or blame
Go for a Burton – die
Go west – die
Imshi! – Shoo! *or* Go away!
Jankers – punishment
Jildi – hurry up
Kip – sleep
Mufti – civilian clothes
Pimple – hill
San Ferry Ann – It doesn't matter
Vamoose – Go away *or* Get lost!
Wallah – person
Wipers – the French town of
Ypres

World War Two recipes

• Sugarless apple dessert • Woolton Pie • Rabbit stew • Eggless cake •
• Rumford one-egg cake • Mock fish cakes • • Bread pudding • Syrup loaf •
• Beef hash pudding • Potato floddies • Sour milk pancakes • Trench cake •
• Beehive cake • Anzac buscuits • War cake • Spam fritters • Carrot cookies •

14

Wartime food ration allowance for one adult

Bacon and ham – 4oz
Meat to the value of – 1s 2d
  (eg ½lb minced beef)
Butter – 2oz
Cheese – 2oz
Margarine – 4oz
Cooking fat – 4oz

Milk – 3 pints
Sugar – 8oz
Preserves – 1lb every 2 months
Tea – 2oz
Eggs – 1 fresh egg per week
Sweets – 12oz every 4 weeks

The ration also provided 16 points per adult per month for additional goods such as a tin of fish or 8lb of split peas (both of which cost 16 points).

World War Two poster slogans

Careless Talk Costs Lives • Dig For Victory • Make Do And Mend
Lend A Hand On The Land • Join The Women's Land Army
Look Out In The Blackout • Is Your Journey Really Necessary?
Keep Calm And Carry On • Britain Shall Not Burn
Be Like Dad • Keep Mum!
Hitler Will Send No Warning • Save Kitchen Waste For The Pigs
Coughs And Sneezes Spread Diseases
Mothers, Send Them Out Of London
Don't Take The Squander Bug When You Go Shopping • V For Victory
Women Of Britain • Come Into The Factories • Put That Light OUT!

Woolton Pie: the official recipe

Take 1lb each of diced potatoes, cauliflower, swedes and carrots, three or four spring onions, one teaspoonful of vegetable extract and one teaspoonful of oatmeal.

Cook all together for 10 minutes with just enough water to cover.

Stir occasionally to prevent the mixture from sticking.

Allow to cool; put into a pie dish, sprinkle with chopped parsley and cover with a crust of potatoes or wholemeal pastry.

Bake in a moderate oven until the pastry is nicely brown and serve hot with brown gravy.

When rationing in the UK began and ended

	Rationing introduced	Rationing lifted
Petrol	September 1939	May 1950
Butter	January 1940	May 1954
Bacon	January 1940	July 1954
Ham	January 1940	July 1954
Sugar	January 1940	September 1953
Meat	March 1940	July 1954
Tea	July 1940	October 1952
Margarine and cooking fat	July 1940	May 1954
Cheese	July 1940	May 1954
Jam, marmalade	March 1941	December 1948
Treacle and syrup	March 1941	May 1950
Clothes	June 1941	March 1949
Eggs	June 1941	March 1953
Coal	July 1941	June 1958
Dried fruit	January 1942	May 1950
Soap	February 1942	September 1950
Sweets	July 1942	February 1953
Biscuits	August 1942	May 1950
Bread	July 1946	July 1948
Potatoes	November 1947	April 1948

Quotes from the wartime speeches of Winston Churchill

- I have nothing to offer but blood, toil, tears and sweat. *May 13, 1940*
- We shall defend our island, whatever the cost may be,
  we shall fight on the beaches, we shall fight on the landing grounds,
  we shall fight in the fields and in the streets, we shall fight in the hills;
  we shall never surrender. *June 4, 1940*
- Let us therefore brace ourselves to our duties, and so bear ourselves,
  that if the British Empire and its Commonwealth last for a thousand
  years, men will still say, "This was their finest hour." *June 18, 1940*
- Never in the field of human conflict was so much owed by so many
  to so few. *August 20, 1940*
- Now this is not the end. It is not even the beginning of the end.
  But it is, perhaps, the end of the beginning. *November 10, 1942*

Nicknames

Aggie – Person with the surname "Weston"
(from Dame Aggie Weston, a pioneer of the temperance movement).

Annie Laurie – Female lorry driver.

Balls – Person with the surname "Ivory"
(because billiard balls were made from ivory).

Bella – Loud-voiced woman.

Betsy – Person with the surname "Gay"
(from the music hall song Charming Betsy Gay).

Billy – Person with the surname "Wells"
(from the boxer Bombardier Billy Wells).

Bubbles – Child with curly hair
(from the Pears soap advertisement).

Chalky – Person with the surname "White".

Chippy – Person with the surname "Carpenter".

Conky – Person with a large nose.

Daisy – Person with the surname "Bell"
(from the song "Daisy Bell").

Eno's – A know-all (from Eno's Fruit Salts).

Gipsy – Person with the surname "Lee".

Half-pint – Person of diminutive stature.

Knobby – Person with the surname "Cole"
(from "a knob of coal").

Nippy – A waitress (registered in 1924
as a trade mark by J Lyons & Co Ltd).

Nobby – Person with the surname "Clarke"
(because clerks were required to wear suits
normally worn by the upper classes, or "nobs", for work.

Nosher – Person who eats (or noshes) between meals.

Smudger – Person with the surname "Smith"
(from the smudges of soot found in a blacksmith's forge).

Snowball – Person with fair hair.

Spider – Person with the surname "Webb".

Spud – Person with surname "Murphy"
(because of Irish connections).

Skipping rhymes

Salt, mustard, vinegar, pepper
French almond rock.
Bread and butter for our supper,
That's all mother's got.
Eggs and bacon, salted herring,
Pease pudding in a pot,
Pickled onions, apple pudding,
We will eat the lot.
Mabel, Mabel, lay the table
Don't forget the salt, mustard, vinegar, pepper...

I'm a Girl Guide
Dressed in blue.
These are the actions I must do
Salute to the King
And bow to the Queen
And turn right round on a lump of string.

On the mountain stands a lady
Who she is I do not know
All she wants is gold and silver
All she wants is a nice young man
So I call in my very best friend and that is...

Teddy Bear, Teddy Bear, turn around,
Teddy Bear, Teddy Bear, touch the ground
Teddy Bear, Teddy Bear, touch your shoe
Teddy Bear, Teddy Bear, that will do!

Teddy Bear, Teddy Bear, go upstairs
Teddy Bear, Teddy Bear, say your prayers
Teddy Bear, Teddy Bear, turn out the lights
Teddy Bear, Teddy Bear, say good-night!

Apples, peaches, pears and plums
Tell me when your birthday comes.

The Beano

The first issue of *The Beano* was dated Tuesday, July 30, 1938 and priced at 2d. It contained the following:

Front cover strip:	Back cover:
Big Eggo (the ostrich)	Tin Can Tommy ("The Clockwork Boy")
Ping the Elastic Man	Wee Peem ("He's a proper scream!")
Brave Captain Kipper	Hairy Dan ("How Dan won the race with his hairy face")
Morgyn the Mighty	Contrary Mary ("You can't play a joke on Mary the Moke")
Helpful Henry	Little Dead-Eye Dick ("He's a fun man and he's a gun man")
Tom Thumb	Black Flash the Beaver
	Lord Snooty and His Pals ("Son of a duke but always pally / With the Beezer Kids of Ash-Can Alley")

Over the next few years the following strips appeared:

Pansy Potter the Strongman's Daughter (1938-93)
Dennis the Menace (1951-present)
Frosty McNab (1938-41)
Kat and Kanary (1952-58)
Wild Boy of the Woods (1938-58)
Roger the Dodger (1953-present)
Doubting Thomas (1940-42)
Little Plum (1953-2006)
Musso the Wop (1940-43)
Minnie the Minx (1953-present)
The Magic Lollipop (1941-51)
The Bash Street Kids (1954-present – originally called *"When The Bell Rings"*)
The Shipwrecked Circus (1943-58)
General Jumbo (1953-75)
Jimmy and His Magic Patch (1944-59)

Jonah (1958-63)
Strang the Terrible (1944-45)
The Three Bears (1959-present)
Sammy Shrinko (1946-48)
The Great Flood of London (1960-61)
Maxy's Taxi (1947-51)
Colonel Crackpot's Circus (1960-63)
Deep-Sea Danny's Iron Fish (1949-67)
The Q Bikes (1963-71)
Biffo the Bear (1948-1986)
Billy Whizz (1964-2007)
Ding Dong Belle (1949-51)
Billy the Cat (1967-74)
Jack Flash (1949-58)
Pup Parade (1967-88)
Have-a-Go Joe (1949-51)
The Nibblers (1970-84)
Red Rory of the Eagles (1951-62)
Baby-Face Finlayson (1972-2005)

Proverbs

A bad penny always comes back

A bad workman blames his tools.

A bird in the hand is worth two in the bush.

A cold hand and a warm heart.

A drowning man will clutch at a straw.

A fair exchange is no robbery

A fool and his money are soon parted.

A friend in need is a friend indeed.

A man is known by the company he keeps.

A penny saved is a penny earned.

A rolling stone gathers no moss.

A stitch in time saves nine.

A watched pot never boils.

A woman's work is never done.

A wonder lasts but nine days.

Actions speak louder than words.

All is fair in love and war.

All roads lead to Rome.

All things come to those who wait.

All work and no play makes Jack a dull boy.

An apple a day keeps the doctor away.

An Englishman's home is his castle.

As well be hanged for a sheep as a lamb.

As you make your bed, so must you lie on it.

Ask no questions and you'll be told no lies.

Beauty is but skin-deep.

Beggars cannot be choosers.

Better the devil you know than the devil you don't know.

Better be safe than sorry.

Birds of a feather flock together.

Blood is thicker than water.

Charity begins at home.

Children should be seen and not heard.

Cut your coat according to your cloth.

Discretion is the better part of valour.

Don't count your chickens
before they're hatched.

Don't spoil the ship for a ha'p'orth of tar.

Early to bed and early to rise makes a man
healthy, wealthy, and wise

Every cloud has a silver lining.

Every dog has his day.

Faint heart never won fair lady.

Great minds think alike.

Handsome is as handsome does.

He who laughs last laughs longest.

He who pays the piper may call the tune.

Here today and gone tomorrow.

If ifs and ands were pots and pans,
there'd be no need for tinkers.

If the mountain will not come to Mohammed,
Mohammed must go to the mountain.

In the country of the blind

the one-eyed man is king.

It never rains but it pours.

It takes all sorts to make a world.

It takes two to make a quarrel.

It's an ill wind that blows nobody good.

It's never too late to learn.

Jack of all trades, master of none.

Least said, soonest mended.

Let bygones be bygones.

Let sleeping dogs lie.

Little things please little minds.

Look before you leap.

Love will find a way.

Lucky at cards, unlucky in love.

Make a virtue of necessity.

Make hay while the sun shines.

Make the best of a bad bargain.

Many a mickle makes a muckle.

Many a true word spoken in jest.

Many hands make light work.

More haste, less speed.

Necessity is the mother of invention.

Needs must when the devil drives.

Never judge by appearances.

Never put off till tomorrow
what can be done today.

There is no fool like an old fool.

No news is good news.

No rose without a thorn.

Of two evils, choose the lesser.

Once bitten, twice shy.

One good turn deserves another.

One hour's sleep before midnight
is worth two after.

One law for the rich and another for the poor.

One man's meat is another's poison.

One swallow does not make a summer.

Out of sight, out of mind.

Out of the frying pan into the fire.

Penny wise, pound foolish.

People who live in glass houses
should not throw stones.

Possession is nine-tenths of the law.

Practice makes perfect.

Practise what you preach.

Prevention is better than cure.

Pride goes before a fall.

Pride often borrows the cloak of humility.

Procrastination is the thief of time.

Rain before seven, fine before eleven.

Rats desert a sinking ship.

Red sky at night, shepherd's delight;
red sky in the morning, shepherd's warning.

Revenge is sweet.

Proverbs continued

Rome was not built in a day.
Save your breath to cool your porridge.
Scratch a Russian and you'll find a Tartar.
Spare the rod and spoil the child.
Sticks and stones may break my bones
but names will never hurt me.
Still waters run deep.
Stolen fruit is sweetest.
Take care of the pennies and the pounds
will take care of themselves.
Talk of the devil and he'll appear.
The early bird catches the worm.
The end justifies the means.
The first step is the hardest.
The game is not worth the candle.
The grass is greener on the other side of the fence.
The proof of the pudding is in the eating.
The road to hell is paved with good intentions.
There are none so blind as those who won't see.
There's honour among thieves.
There's no time like the present.
There's no smoke without fire.
There's many a slip betwixt cup and lip.

To err is human, to forgive divine.
Too many cooks spoil the broth.
Truth is stranger than fiction.
Two heads are better than one.
Two wrongs don't make a right.
Walls have ears.
Waste not, want not.
What's bred in the bone comes out in the flesh.
What's sauce for the goose is sauce for the gander.
What the eye doesn't see, the heart doesn't grieve over.
Whatever's worth doing is worth doing well.
When in Rome, do as the Romans do.
When one door shuts, another opens.
When the cat's away, the mice will play.
Where there's a will there's a way.
While there's life there's hope.
Who sups with the devil needs a long spoon.
Worse things happen at sea.
You can take a horse to water,
but you can't make him drink.
You can't teach an old dog new tricks.
You must take the fat with the lean.
You never know what you can do till you try.

Years food items were introduced in the UK

1930   Sliced bread began to appear.

1937   Spam first sold (originally known as Hormel Spiced Ham).

1939   Instant coffee – Nescafé – was first introduced. Originally sold in tins, the brown jars appeared in 1961. Maxwell House coffee launched in 1954.

1946   Frozen vegetables; the first sold in the UK were Birds Eye frozen peas. Birds Eye sold 390 tons of frozen peas in 1946. Presumably the peas were thawed out immediately, as people did not have freezers at the time.

1953   Tea bags; Tetley introduced the tea bag to Britain (33 years after Americans had started using them).

1954   US company Swanson introduced the TV dinner in the UK.

1955   Birds Eye frozen fish fingers were first sold, at 1s 8d per pack.

1960   Golden Wonder introduced Ready Salted crisps. These were followed up with the first flavoured crisps in 1962 (Cheese and Onion being the first flavour sold). Previously crisps had come with a separate blue bag of salt.

1963   Ski fruit flavour yogurts were first sold in urn-shaped pots.

UK political leaders 1945-90

Year	Prime Minister	Chancellor of the Exchequer	Foreign Secretary	Home Secretary	Leader of the House of Commons
1945-51	Clement Attlee	Hugh Dalton	Ernest Bevin	James Chuter Ede	Herbert Morrison
		Stafford Cripps	Herbert Morrison		James Chuter Ede
		Hugh Gaitskell			
1951-55	Sir Winston Churchill	Rab Butler	Sir Anthony Eden	Sir David Maxwell-Fyfe	Harry Crookshank
				Gwilym Lloyd George	
1955-57	Sir Anthony Eden	Rab Butler	Harold Macmillan	Gwilym Lloyd George	Rab Butler
		Harold Macmillan	Selwyn Lloyd		
1957-63	Harold Macmillan	Peter Thorneycroft	Selwyn Lloyd	Rab Butler	Rab Butler
		Derick Heathcoat-Amory	Earl of Home	Henry Brooke	Iain Macleod
		Selwyn Lloyd			
		Reginald Maudling			
1963-64	Sir Alec Douglas-Home	Reginald Maudling	Rab Butler	Henry Brooke	Selwyn Lloyd
1964-70	Harold Wilson	James Callaghan	Patrick Gordon Walker	Frank Soskice	Herbert Bowden
		Roy Jenkins	Michael Stewart	Roy Jenkins	Richard Crossman
			George Brown	James Callaghan	Fred Peart
			Michael Stewart		
1970-74	Edward Heath	Iain Macleod	Sir Alec Douglas-Home	Reginald Maudling	William Whitelaw
		Anthony Barber		Robert Carr	Robert Carr
					James Prior
1974-76	Harold Wilson	Denis Healey	James Callaghan	Roy Jenkins	Edward Short
1976-79	James Callaghan	Denis Healey	Anthony Crosland	Roy Jenkins	Michael Foot
			David Owen	Merlyn Rees	
1979-90	Margaret Thatcher	Geoffrey Howe	Lord Carrington	William Whitelaw	Norman St John-Stevas
		Nigel Lawson	Francis Pym	Leon Brittan	Francis Pym
		John Major	Geoffrey Howe	Douglas Hurd	John Biffen
		Norman Lamont	John Major	David Waddington	John Wakeham
			Douglas Hurd		Geoffrey Howe

The price of a stamp

In 1900 the price of a stamp was 1d (0.4p) for inland post.
In the middle of the 20th century, inland postage rates went up as follows:

	1937-40	1940-49	1949-51	1952
Letter	1 ½d	2 ½d	2 ½d	2 ½d
Postcard	1d	2d	2d	2d
Printed papers	½d	1d	1 ½d	1 ½d
Registration	3d	3d	4d	6d
Express delivery	6d	6d	6d	6d

In 1965 inland rates were:

- 4d for a letter up to 2oz
- 6d for a letter up to 4oz
- 3d for a small postcard
- 4d for a large postcard
- 6d for recorded delivery
- 3s for special delivery

In 1968 first and second class postage was introduced. The rates were:

- First class: 5d for up to 4oz
- First class: 9d for up to 6oz
- Second class: 4d for up to 4oz
- Second class: 6d for up to 6oz

In 1971 following decimalization the rates were changed again and increased as follows:

	1975	1980	1990	2000	2006	2011
First class	8.5p	10p	20p	26p	32p	46p
Second class	6.5p	8p	15p	19p	23p	36p

Demob issue

As made from Quartermaster's Stores for servicemen at the end of WW2.

Civilian suit	Hat
Shirt	Two collars
Tie	Pair of shoes
Two pairs of socks	Two pairs of underpants
Mackintosh	Two studs
Pair of cufflinks	*all issued in a flat cardboard box.*

Women could have a demob suit or £12 10s plus 56 clothing coupons.
The government calculated this would buy:

Hat (10s)	Suit or dress (£4 15s)
Scarf (6s)	Blouse or jumper (£1)
Stockings (10s)	Shoes (£1 5s)
Raincoat (£3 10s)	*which left 14s for alterations.*

ITMA characters and catchphrases

The BBC radio comedy series *ITMA* entertained British audiences from 1939
and through the war until the death of its star Tommy Handley in 1949.
The cast included Fred Yule, Clarence Wright, Molly Weir, Hattie Jacques,
Deryck Guyler, Jack Train, Maurice Denham, Clarence Wright, Dorothy
Summers and Horace Percival, and the show's characters included:

Colonel Chinstrap	*("I don't mind if I do, sir!"),*
Mrs Mopp, the office char	*("Can I do yer now, sir?"),*
Removal men Claude and Cecil	*("After you, Claude" "No, after you, Cecil"),*
German spy Fünf	*("This is Fünf speaking"),*
The diver	*("Don't forget the diver, sir"),*
Ali Oop	*("I go – I come back again")*
Mona Lott	*("It's being so cheerful as keeps me going").*

TTFN

Captains of the England cricket team since the war

Years during which they captained Test sides shown in brackets.

Wally Hammond (1938-47)
Norman Yardley (1946-50)
Ken Cranston (1947-48)
George Mann (1948-49)
Freddie Brown (1949-51)
Nigel Howard (1951-52)
Donald Carr (1951-52)
Len Hutton (1952-55)
David Sheppard (1954)
Peter May (1955-61)
Colin Cowdrey (1959-69)
Ted Dexter (1961-64)
M J K Smith (1963-66)
Brian Close (1966-67)
Tom Graveney (1968)
Ray Illingworth (1969-73)
Tony Lewis (1972-73)
Mike Denness (1973-75)
John Edrich (1974-75)
Tony Greig (1975-77)
Mike Brearley (1977-81)

Geoffrey Boycott (1977-78)
Ian Botham (1980-81)
Keith Fletcher (1981-82)
Bob Willis (1982-84)
David Gower (1982-89)
Mike Gatting (1986-88)
John Emburey (1988)
Chris Cowdrey (1988)
Graham Gooch (1988-93)
Allan Lamb (1989-91)
Alec Stewart (1992-2001)
Michael Atherton (1993-2001)
Nasser Hussain (1999-2003)
Mark Butcher (1999)
Michael Vaughan (2003-08)
Marcus Trescothick (2004-06)
Andrew Flintoff (2006-07)
Andrew Strauss (2006-11)
Kevin Pietersen (2008-09)
Alastair Cook (2010)

Essential school classroom equipment

Pupils   Set square; ruler (in inches, of course);
protractor; dividers; log book (i.e. book of logarithms);
inkwell; blotting paper; ink pellets; pencil box;
eraser with white half for pencil and red half for ink.

Teachers   Chalk!; blackboard eraser (for occasional use as missile);
the cane; red pen; the register.

How to make the perfect cup of tea

- Use loose tea which should be stored in an airtight container at room temperature.
- Fill kettle with sufficient fresh water.
- Heat water until it is absolutely boiling.
- Warm the tea pot.
- Using a clean dry measure, add 1tsp of tea for each cup of tea to be served plus 1tsp "for the pot".
- Allow the tea to brew for 2–5 minutes.
- Add milk to cups before pouring tea.
- Stir the pot and pour tea into cups using a strainer.

You didn't have a fridge?

How the percentage of people in England with domestic appliances leapt between the war and the mid 1960s.

	% homes with in 1945	% homes with in mid-60s
Electric iron	65%	94%
Fridge	2%	46%
Telephone	21%	35%
Television	0.25%	85%
Vacuum cleaner	32%	81%
Washing machine	3%	58%

The Queen's residences (from north to south)

Balmoral Castle, Aberdeenshire; Holyrood Palace, Edinburgh; Sandringham House, Norfolk; the Savoy Chapel, London; The Tower of London; Clarence House, London; Kensington Palace, London; the Banqueting House, Whitehall, London; Buckingham Palace, London; Frogmore House, Windsor, Berkshire; Windsor Castle, Berkshire; Hampton Court Palace, Richmond upon Thames.

Surname pronunciations

Name	Pronunciation	Name	Pronunciation
Bagehot	Badge Ut	Geogehan	Gay Gun
Beauchamp	Bee chum	Harewood	Har Wud
Belvoir	Beaver	Hiscox	Hizzko
Berkeley	Bark Lee	Howick	Hoyk
Buccleuch	Buc-loo	Leveson-Gower	Loosen Gore
Caius	Keys	Mainwaring	Mannering
Chandos	Shan Doss	Marjoribanks	Marchbanks
Cholmondley	Chumley	Menzies	Min Giss
Cockburn	Coburn	Ruthven	Rivven
Coke	Cook	St Clair	Sink Lur
Colquhoun	Ca hoon	St John	Sin Jun
Cowper	Cooper	St Paul	Sem Pul
Crichton	Cry Tun	Taliaferro	Talliver
Dalziel	Deal or Dee El	Tyrwhitt	Tirrit
Darlingscot	Darscot	Urquhart	Ur Cut
Featherstonehaugh	Fan Shaw, Fest Uhn Haw, Fee Suhn Hay, Feer Stuhn Haw or Feather Stun Haw	Woolfhardisworthy	Wool Zee
Fuchs	Fooks	Wriotheseley	Riz-lee, Rottsly, Rittslee, Rithly or Wriotheseley

Advertising slogans from our youth: aftershave

- The classic, masculine fragrance. The mark of a man (Old Spice).
- Old Spice! Refreshing, invigorating, sensual! Perhaps it's one reason why women are always impatiently waiting for their men to return from the sea! (Old Spice).
- Splash it all over! (Brut).
- Mandate says a lot for a man! (Mandate aftershave).
- For men who don't have to try too hard (Denim).
- Be careful how you use it! (Hai Karate).

Imperial weights

1 drachm = $1/16$ ounce.

1 ounce = about 28.35 gm (from the Latin uncia meaning $1/12$ of a pound, as there were 12 ounces in the ancient Roman pound).

1 pound = 16 ounces (the Roman pound was the libra – hence the abbreviation lb for pound).

1 stone = 14 pounds.

1 quarter = 2 stone.

1 hundredweight = 8 stones or 112 pounds (although people very rarely quote their bodyweight in hundredweight).

1 ton = 20 hundredweight or 160 stones or 2,240 pounds (derives from the word "tun", meaning a large barrel – see below).

Imperial liquid measurements

1 fluid ounce = $1/20$th pint or $1/160$th gallon (28.41 ml).

1 gill = ¼ pint (142.06 ml).

1 pint = $1/8$th gallon or 20 fluid ounces (568.26 ml).

1 quart = 2 pints (1,136 ml).

1 gallon = 8 pints (4,546 ml); the gallon was based on the volume of 10lb of water at a temperature of 62° Fahrenheit.

Brewery casks

1 firkin = 9 gallons, from the Middle Dutch "vierdekijn" meaning a quarter – there being 4 firkins in a barrel.

1 kilderkin = 2 firkins.

1 barrel = 4 firkins or 36 gallons.

1 hogshead = 1½ barrels or 6 firkins or 54 gallons.

1 butt = 2 hogsheads or 3 barrels or 12 firkins or 108 gallons.

1 tun = 4 hogsheads or 6 barrels or 24 firkins or 216 gallons.

Correct forms of verbal address when meeting members of the royal family

The Queen:

On introduction:	A bow of the head or a discreet, dignified curtsy.
Initial address:	Your Majesty.
Subsequent address:	Ma'am (pronounced "mam" not "maarm").

Other members of the royal family:

Initial address:	Your Royal Highness.
Subsequent address:	Sir or ma'am.

Useful Latin phrases

Errare humanum est (to err is human).

Memento mori (remember that you will die).

Mens sana in corpore sano (a healthy mind in a healthy body).

Ipsa scientia potestas est (knowledge itself is power).

Nil desperandum (never despair).

Qui audet adipiscitur (he who dares wins).

Dum vita est spes est (while there's life, there's hope).

Amor vincit omnia (love conquers all).

Audaces fortuna iuvat (fortune favours the brave).

Cogito ergo sum (I think, therefore I am).

Veni, vidi, vici (I came, I saw, I conquered).

Die dulci freure (have a nice day).

Iconic trains: the Flying Scotsman

- Perhaps the most famous steam locomotive of all.
- Designed by Sir Nigel Gresley in 1938.
- Had a top speed of 100mph.
- Ran between London and Edinburgh.
- It pulled into the yard for the final time in 1963.

Rhymes for selection in playground games

Eeny meeny miny mo
Catch a tiger by the toe
If he hollers, let him go
Eeny meeny miny mo.

Ip dip, dog s**t
You are not it.

One potato, two potato
Three potato, four
Five potato, six potato
Seven potato – more!
(This involved putting out your "spuds" – clenched fists).

Ibble obble, black bobble
Ibble obble out!

Ip dip dip, sky blue
Who's it? Not you!

And not forgetting Stone, Paper, Scissors, in which children formed a ring, put their hands into the middle in the shape of one of the above and were eliminated if their choice was beaten by the others, i.e. stone blunts scissors, paper wraps up stone, scissors cut paper.

Cigarettes you may have smoked behind the bicycle sheds

Albany • Anchor • Black Cat • Cadets • Cambridge • Capstan Full Strength
Consulate • Embassy Regal • Gallaher • Gauloises • Guards • Joysticks
Kensitas • Kool • Nelson • Pall Mall • Park Drive • Passing Clouds
Player's No.6 • Player's No.10 • Player's Weights • Piccadilly
Sobranie Black Russian • Sovereign • Senior Service • Woodbine

Mackintosh's

Mackintosh's was founded in Halifax in 1890. Violet Mackintosh developed Mackintosh's Celebrated Toffee which blended traditional brittle butterscotch with softer American caramel. Mackintosh's products included:

Quality Street: First produced 1936. The name was taken from a 1901 play by J.M. Barrie, while the illustrations on the box were inspired by the play's main characters.

Rolo: Launched in 1937, priced at 2d for "a roll of delicious creamy chocolate toffee croquettes".

Mackintosh's also launched Toffo in 1939, Munchies in 1957, Caramac in 1959, Good News in 1960, Toffee Crisp in 1963 and Golden Cup in 1967.

Old brands of tea

Barbers Tea.
Lyons Quick Brew Tea ("saves one for the pot").
Lyons Hornimans Tea.
Lyons Family Favourite Tea.
Lyons Blue, Yellow, Red or Green Label.
Lyons Small Leaf Tea.
Brooke Bond Dividend ("Cut out this coupon – every time you fill a Brooke Bond dividend card you get 5/-").
Brooke Bond Choicest ("a blend of the choicest teas procurable – served in the Brooke Bond Board Room").
Number Ninety-Nine Tea ("the real leaf edge and tip").
Ty-Phoo Tea ("the tea that doctors recommend").

BBC newsreaders of the 1950s, '60s & '70s

Robert Dougall • Kenneth Kendall
Michael Aspel • Richard Baker • Corbet Woodall
Peter Woods • Richard Whitmore

Festival of Britain exhibits

After the war we all needed cheering up and so the Festival of Britain was held on the South Bank of the Thames between May and September 1951 – a hundred years after the Great Exhibition of the Victorian era.

The Dome of Discovery – 93 feet high and 365 feet across and containing exhibitions on outer space, the sea and the Earth.

The Skylon – futuristic, cigar-shaped, UFO-like construction put up near the Dome of Discovery. Wags at the time commented that, like the British economy, the Skylon had no visible means of support!

The Telekinema – situated near Waterloo station, for the showing of both TV and cinema films, including some in 3D. After the festival it became the home of the new National Film Theatre.

The Royal Festival Hall – the only Festival of Britain buildings not pulled down by Winston Churchill's incoming Conservative government.

Far Tottering and Oyster Creek Railway – inspired by the Punch cartoons of Roland Emett, ran through Battersea Pleasure Gardens.

Festival Pleasure Gardens – tree walk, fun fair and the Guinness clock.

MV Campania – ship that carried a travelling version of the South Bank exhibition to ports including Plymouth, Hull, Belfast, Bristol, Dundee, Newcastle, Cardiff, Glasgow and Birkenhead.

The Lansbury Estate – public housing estate in Poplar demonstrating modern town planning ideas, named after Poplar councillor and Labour MP George Lansbury.

3D films shown at the Telekinema at the Festival of Britain

Royal River (depicting a boat trip up the Thames).
The Black Swan (a ballet film).
The Owl And The Pussycat (animated film by Halas and Batchelor).
A Solid Explanation (a demonstration of stereoscopy).

The coronation of HM Queen Elizabeth II

Date of coronation	Tuesday, June 2, 1953.
Time of service	11.15 am to 2.00 pm.
Place	Westminster Abbey.
Weather	Wet!
Age of queen at coronation	27 years and 6 weeks.
Crowned as	Queen of the United Kingdom, Canada, Australia, New Zealand, South Africa, Ceylon and Pakistan, and Head of the Commonwealth.
Ceremony conducted by	Archbishop of Canterbury, Geoffrey Fisher.
Number of guests at Abbey	8,251.
Recipe for coronation oil used to anoint the new monarch	Secret – but it contains oils of orange flowers, roses, jasmine, cinnamon, musk, civet and ambergris.

Flowers embroidered on Her Majesty's coronation dress

Tudor rose of England, Scots thistle, Welsh leek, Irish shamrock, Australian wattle, Canadian maple leaf, New Zealand fern, South African protea, Indian and Ceylonese lotus flowers, Pakistani wheat, cotton and jute, and four-leaf clover.

Dates of the 10 previous coronations

George VI	May 12, 1937	George V	June 22, 1911
Edward VII	August 9, 1902	Victoria	June 28, 1838
William IV	September 8, 1831	George IV	July 19, 1821
George III	September 22, 1761	George II	October 11, 1727
George I	October 20, 1714	Anne	April 23, 1702

Peacetime National Service

Introduced	January 1, 1949 (by the 1948 National Service Act).
Period of service	18 months (plus 4 years in the reserves), increased in 1950 to 2 years (plus 3½ years in the reserves).
Final call-up	December 31, 1960.
Eligible for call-up	Healthy males aged 17 to 21.
Exemptions	Workers in "essential services" (coal-mining, farming, Merchant Navy); conscientious objectors; those born after October 1, 1939; people from Northern Ireland; those standing for parliament.
Likely postings	West Germany, Palestine, Aden and the Suez Canal Zone, Cyprus, Hong Kong, Singapore, Malaya, Korea.
Basic pay (in 1949)	28 shillings a week.
Leave	14 days for every 8 months of service.

Words spelt differently in British and American English

	British	USA
	Catalogue	Catalog
	Centre	Center
	Colour	Color
	Flavour	Flavor
	Humour	Humor
	Licence	License
	Litre	Liter
	Neighbour	Neighbor
	Theatre	Theater

The clothes we wore

1950s

Boys: short back and sides, crew cut or pudding basin haircut, grey socks, sandals or plimsolls, khaki or grey shorts, Fair Isle pullover.

Girls: pigtails, cotton dress, navy-blue knickers, buttoned cardigan and shoes with straps or plimsolls.

Teenage boys: greased hair, "drainpipe" trousers, checked shirt, velvet-collared jacket, bootlace tie, "slim Jim" tie, "winklepicker" shoes.

Teenage girls: "beehive" hairdo, cotton dress, stockings, stiletto shoes.

Men: old demob suit, shirt with detachable collar, tie, brogues.

Women: perm, twinset, high-heeled shoes, headscarf or hat.

1960s

Boys: slightly longer and ungreased versions of 1950s haircut, polo shirt, T-shirt, "snake" loop belt.

Girls: longer hair, brighter colours.

Teenage boys: "Beatle" cut, then long hair or skinhead cut, "shortie" raincoat, kipper tie, Cuban heel boots, tab-collar shirt, kaftan, flares, blue jeans, "granny" specs, parka.

Teenage girls: short "Twiggy" style or "Julie Driscoll" hair, "Op art" patterned dress, kaftan, miniskirt, "maxi" dress.

Men: suit, bowler hat, trilby, flat cap, fawn raincoat, sports jacket.

Women: slightly shorter skirt, lower-heeled shoes.

1970s

Boys: longer hair or skinhead haircut, tank tops, jeans, trainers.

Girls: hair short on top and long at the back, bell-bottom trousers, Bay City Rollers scarf.

Teenage boys: very long hair or skinhead haircut, perm, a Mohican, bomber jacket, jeans, trainers or "bovver" boots, boiler suit, safety pins, skinny tie.

Teenage girls: perm or long hair, hot pants, clogs, wedge-heeled shoes, wide-brimmed hats.

Men: longer hair, sideboards, moustache, kipper tie.

Women: longer hair, Laura Ashley dresses, floppy hats.

Latin declensions

First declension

	Male nouns		Female nouns	
	Singular	**Plural**	**Singular**	**Plural**
Nominative	agricola	agricolae	puella	puellae
Vocative	agricola	agricolae	puella	puellae
Accusative	agricolam	agricolas	puellam	puellas
Genitive	agricolae	agricolarum	puellae	puellarum
Dative	agricolae	agricolis	puellae	puellis
Ablative	agricola	agricolis	puella	puellis

agricola = a farmer   puella = a girl

Second declension

	Male nouns		Neuter nouns	
	Singular	**Plural**	**Singular**	**Plural**
Nominative	dominus	domini	bellum	bella
Vocative	domine	domini	bellum	bella
Accusative	dominum	dominos	bellum	bella
Genitive	domini	dominorum	belli	bellorum
Dative	domino	dominis	bello	bellis
Ablative	domino	dominis	bello	bellis

dominus = lord   bellum = war

Third declension

	Male nouns		Neuter nouns	
	Singular	**Plural**	**Singular**	**Plural**
Nominative	rex	reges	opus	opera
Vocative	rex	reges	opus	opera
Accusative	regem	reges	opus	opera
Genitive	regis	regum	operis	operum
Dative	regis	regibus	operis	operibus
Ablative	rege	regibus	opere	operibus

rex = king   opus = work

Nominative: the subject of the verb.
Vocative: used when calling or addressing someone or something.
Accusative: the object of a verb.
Genitive: used to express the noun's possession of something.
Dative: the indirect object, nouns that something is done to or for.
Ablative: nouns that are by, with or from something.

Average earnings in the UK since 1950

	Gross weekly earnings	Gross earnings per annum		Gross weekly earnings	Gross earnings per annum
1950	£7.08	£368.16	1980	£111.20	£5,782.40
1955	£10.55	£548.60	1985	£171.00	£8,892.00
1960	£13.69	£711.88	1990	£263.10	£13,681.20
1965	£18.36	£954.72	1995	£337.60	£17,555.20
1970	£26.10	£1,357.20	2000	£419.70	£21,824.40
1975	£54.00	£2,808.00	2005	£516.40	£26,852.80

The average cost of a house in the UK

	Average price of house in UK	% increase from 1945 price	As % of 2011 price
1945	£545	0	0.34
1950	£1,940	256	1.21
1955	£2,064	279	1.29
1960	£2,530	364	1.58
1965	£3,660	572	2.28
1970	£4,975	813	3.10
1975	£11,787	2,063	7.35
1980	£23,596	4,230	14.71
1985	£31,103	5,607	19.39
1990	£59,785	10,870	37.27
1995	£65,644	11,945	40.93
2000	£101,550	18,533	63.31
2005	£151,757	27,745	94.61
2011	£160,395	29,330	100.00

Items from the home medicine cabinet

- Phillips Milk of Magnesia *(antacid laxative "to avoid flatulence and pain after meals")*.

- Fynnon Salt *("The best thing I've ever taken for rheumatism. Some call it rheumatism. Some call it fibrositis. Whatever it was, I'm rid of it – and very glad I had the sense to take Fynnon Salt!")*

- Eno's Fruit Salt *(pleasant, cooling, health-giving effervescent saline – for those with digestive problems and upset bowels).*

- Bile Beans *(vegetable pills for those feeling tired, liverish, constipated, sluggish – also recommended to help keep a slender figure and to prevent unwanted fat forming).*

- Dewitts Kidney and Bladder Pills *(for rheumatism, backache, joint pains, lumbago or any urinary irregularities).*

- Carter's Little Liver Pills *("Cure all liver ills. For headache, dizziness, biliousness, torpid liver, constipation, sallow skin, complexion.")*

- Diuromil *("A glass or two each day, dissolves pain away - a well known and well-tried specific which has for years been used in hospitals and clinics for the speedy relief of pain caused by... rheumatism, fibrositis, lumbago, gout, etc").*

- Vapex Inhalant *("destroys the germs in nose and throat and soon the incipient cold is gone").*

- Cephos *("women turn with confidence to Cephos. Its safe, swift relief of flu, colds, headaches and rheumatism brings it immediately to mind whenever advice is sought. Cephos does not harm the heart.")*

Iconic trains: the Brighton Belle

- Built in 1933.
- Was the world's first electric inter-city train.
- Ran between London Victoria and Brighton.
- Built by Metropolitan Cammell.
- All first-class carriages had women's names:
  Doris, Hazel, Mona, Audrey, Vera and Gwen.

Doing the laundry
(before washing machines)

- Fill the copper (i.e. the large tub in the wash-house) with about 6 full pails of cold water.
- Light a fire beneath the copper.
- When the water is hot, fill the dolly tub (barrel-shaped tub used for washing the clothes).
- Stir the washing in the tub with a wooden dolly peg.
- Once the clothes are clean, feed them through the mangle.
- Then put the clothes in a tin bath filled with clean rinse water.
- Rinse the clothes until the water runs clear.
- Then put the clothes through the mangle again.
- Then peg them out on the line (still dripping wet).

Average life expectancy for those born in the UK through the 20th century

	Males	Females		Males	Females
1901	45.02	48.68	1960	67.83	73.53
1910	51.55	55.19	1970	68.72	74.98
1920	55.65	58.23	1980	70.55	76.59
1930	58.09	62.28	1990	72.86	78.41
1940	57.73	63	2000	75.33	80.13
1950	66.01	70.4			

Car registration years
(letter at end of registration)

A	B	C	D	E	F	G	H	J	K	L
1963	1964	1965	1966	1967	1967	1968	1969	1970	1971	1972

M	N	P	R	S	T	V	W	X	Y
1973	1974	1975	1976	1977	1978	1979	1980	1981	1982

UK airports which were formerly RAF stations

Airport	RAF base name
Bournemouth International Airport	RAF Hurn
Bristol Airport	RAF Lulsgate Bottom
Cardiff Airport	RAF Rhoose
Carlisle Airport	RAF Crosby on Eden
City of Derry Airport	RAF Eglinton
Coventry Airport	RAF Baginton
East Midlands Airport	RAF Castle Donington
Exeter International Airport	RAF Exeter
Fairoaks Airport	RAF Fairoaks
Farnborough Airport	RAF Farnborough
George Best Belfast City Airport	RAF Sydenham
Glasgow International Airport	RAF Abbotsinch
Kent International Airport	RAF Manston
Leeds Bradford International Airport	RAF Yeadon
Liverpool John Lennon Airport	RAF Speke
London Gatwick Airport	RAF Gatwick
London Southend Airport	RAF Rochford
London Stansted Airport	RAF Stansted Mountfitchet
Manchester Airport	RAF Ringway
Newcastle International Airport	RAF Woolsington
Norwich International Airport	RAF Horsham St Faith
Oxford Airport	RAF Kidlington
Robin Hood Airport Doncaster Sheffield	RAF Finningley
Swansea Airport	RAF Fairwood Common

The school day as we knew it: assembly

- This involved the entire school sitting in rows in the school hall.
- There would be the singing of hymns and saying of prayers.
- There would also be an uplifting speech by the head.
- It would often be the forum for naming people who were to be caned.

Old wives' tales

- A black cat crossing your path brings bad luck.
- Breaking a mirror brings seven years' bad luck.
- Cracking your knuckles will give you arthritis.
- Crossing two knives is bad luck.
- Don't pull faces or cross your eyes, or the wind will change and you'll stay like that.
- Don't trust people whose eyes are too close together.
- Eating carrots helps you see in the dark.
- Eating fish makes you brainy.
- Eating your greens will make your hair go curly.
- Feed a cold, starve a fever.
- If two women pour from the same teapot, one of them will have a baby within a year.
- If you bite your tongue while eating, you have recently told a lie.
- If you go out with wet hair, you'll catch a cold.
- If you shiver, it means that someone is walking over your grave.
- If you spill salt, you must throw some over your shoulder for good luck.
- If you swallow chewing gum, it will get wrapped round your tonsils.
- If you swallow an apple pip, a tree will grow in your stomach.
- If your right palm is itchy, you will be coming into money.
- If your left palm is itchy, you'll be paying out money.
- Killing a bee is bad luck.
- Killing a spider will make it rain the next day.
- Only eat shellfish when there's an "r" in the month.
- Opening an umbrella indoors will bring bad luck.
- Sitting on a cold surface will give you piles.
- Sitting too close to the TV will ruin your eyesight.
- Smoking stunts your growth.
- Stepping on pavement cracks means the witches will get you.
- Swimming with a full stomach will give you stomach cramps.
- Walking under a ladder brings bad luck.

And of course:

- If you don't stop doing that, you'll go blind!

Royal births

Prince Philip of Greece and Denmark	June 10, 1921
Princess Elizabeth Alexandra Mary of York (later Queen Elizabeth II)	April 21, 1926
Princess Margaret Rose of York	August 21, 1930
Prince Charles Philip Arthur George	November 14, 1948
Princess Anne Elizabeth Alice Louise	August 15, 1950
Prince Andrew Albert Christian Edward	February 19, 1960
Prince Edward Antony Richard Louis	March 10, 1964
Prince William Arthur Philip Louis	June 21, 1982
Prince Henry Charles Albert David (Prince Harry)	September 15, 1984

Britain's railway companies pre-nationalization

Name	Area	Operation period	
The Great Western Railway	Lon, SW England and Wales	1838-47	Line engineered by Isambard Kingdom Brunel.
London, Midland and Scottish Railway	Well, Lon, Midlands and Scotland	1923-47	largest of the "Big Four".
London and North Eastern Railway	Eastern side of country to Scotland	1923-48	Run for first 16 years by Sir Ralph Wedgwood.
Southern Railway	Lon. to S. coast plus SW and Kent	1923-48	Fleet included the Brighton Belle.

National Service call-up dates of some well-known figures

1949: Ronnie Corbett, Ned Sherrin, Des O'Connor,
Ted Hughes, Colin Dexter

1950: Michael Caine, Peter O'Toole, Arnold Wesker

1951: Michael Aspel

1952: Brian Sewell, Ronnie and Reggie Kray, Brian Epstein,
Michael Frayn, Alan Bennett, Henry Cooper

1954: Nigel Lawson

1955: Michael Parkinson, Tom Baker, Bill Wyman,
Duncan Edwards, Bobby Charlton

1956: Brian Blessed, Richard Wilson, Oliver Reed

1958: Michael Heseltine, Anthony Hopkins

Old electrical wiring colours

Black = neutral; Red = live; Green = earth

NB: This particular combination of colours has not been used since 1971,
so any electrical equipment with this wiring will be at least 40 years old!

UK police ranks

County police forces:
Chief Constable; Deputy Chief Constable; Assistant Chief Constable;
Chief Superintendent; Superintendent; Chief Inspector;
Inspector; Sergeant; Police Constable.
City of London Police:
Commissioner; Assistant Commissioner; Commander; Chief Superintendent;
Superintendent; Chief Inspector; Inspector; Sergeant; Police Constable.
Metropolitan Police:
Commissioner; Deputy Commissioner; Assistant Commissioner;
Deputy Assistant Commissioner; Commander; Chief Superintendent;
Superintendent; Chief Inspector; Inspector; Sergeant; Police Constable.

Advertising slogans from our youth: sweets

- Murray Mints, the too-good-to-hurry mints!
- Don't forget the Fruit Gums, mum! (Rowntree's Fruit Gums).
- Are you a Cadbury's Fruit and Nut case?
- Exotic, delicious, full of Eastern promise!
  (Fry's Turkish Delight).
- Trebor mints are a minty bit stronger!
- The Milky Bar Kid is strong and tough…
- And all because the lady loves Milk Tray…
- Have a break, have a Kit Kat!
- Sixpence-worth of heaven (Cadbury's Flake).
- Only the crumbliest, flakiest chocolate tastes
  like chocolate never tasted before (Cadbury's Flake).
- Smarties – buy some for Lulu!
- A Mars a day helps you work, rest and play!
- Milky Way – the sweet you can eat between meals
  without spoiling your appetite!
- Roses grow on you! (Cadbury's Roses).
- Bridge that gap with Cadbury's Snack!
- If you like a lot of chocolate on your biscuit
  join our club! (Jacob's Club).
- Opal Fruits – made to make your mouth water!
- P-p-pick up a Penguin!
- Pastille pickin' mama (Rowntree's Fruit Pastilles).
- Treets – melt in your mouth, not in your hand.
- The Bounty hunters – they came in search of paradise.
- Sharp's Butter Snap – a name to remember.
- Hands off my Curly Wurly!
- A glass and a half of full cream milk in every half-pound.
  (Cadbury's Dairy Milk).
- Nuts, whole hazelnuts! Cadbury's take 'em
  and they cover them in chocolate! (Cadbury's Whole Nut).
- All the fun of the share (Quality Street).

Traditional ways to read a person's character

Hands

Large hands = strong
Slender hands = weak
Long hands = ingenious
Short hands = careless and foolhardy
Hard hands = bluff
Soft hands = wit
Hairy hands = enjoys luxury
Damp hands = amorous
Cold hands = warm heart

Fingers

Long = artistic
Short = intemperate
Crooked little finger = will become rich

Hair

Lank = cunning
Curly = good natured
Long = strength and good luck

Teeth

Large gap = lucky
Large teeth = physically strong
Small teeth = methodical

Eyes

Dark blue eyes = delicacy
Light blue/ grey eyes = healthy
Green eyes = hardy
Brown eyes = lively

Nose

Big nose = intelligent and determined
Thin nose = jealous and uncertain
Receding nose = obstinate and bad-tempered
Tip-tilted nose = bright and lively

Grand National winners and riders

Year	Horse	Jockey	Trainer
1950	Freebooter	J Power	B Renton
1951	Nickel Coin	J Bullock	J O'Donoghue
1952	Teal	A Thompson	N Crump
1953	Early Mist	B Marshall	V O'Brien
1954	Royal Tan	B Marshall	V O'Brien
1955	Quare Times	P Taaffe	V O'Brien
1956	ESB	D Dick	F Rimell
1957	Sundew	F Winter	F Hudson
1958	Mr Watt	A Freeman	T Taaffe
1959	Oxo	W Stephenson	M Scudamore
1960	Merryman II	G Scott	N Crump
1961	Nicolaus Silver	B Beasley	F Rimell
1962	Kilmore	F Winter	R Price
1963	Ayala	P Buckley	K Piggott
1964	Team Spirit	W Robinson	F Walwyn
1965	Jay Trump	T Smith	F Winter
1966	Anglo 8	T Norman	F Winter
1967	Foinavon	J Buckingham	J Kempton
1968	Red Alligator	B Fletcher	D Smith
1969	Highland Wedding	E Harty	T Balding
1970	Gay Trip	P Taaffe	T Rimmel
1971	Specify	J Cook	J Sutcliffe
1972	Well To Do	G Thorner	T Forster
1973	Red Rum	B Fletcher	D McCain
1974	Red Rum	B Fletcher	D McCain
1975	L'Escargot	T Carberry	D Moore

Threats that might have come your way as a child

I'll box your ears! • I'll tan your hide!
Clear off! • I'll give you what for!
I'll swing for you! • I'll take my belt off to you!
You'll feel the back of my hand in a minute!

Royal weddings

Prince Philip and Princess Elizabeth	November 20, 1947
Princess Margaret and Antony Armstrong-Jones (divorced May 24, 1978)	May 6, 1960
Princess Anne and Captain Mark Phillips (divorced April 23, 1992)	November 14, 1973
Prince Charles and Lady Diana Spencer (divorced August 28, 1996)	July 29, 1981
Prince Andrew and Sarah Ferguson (divorced May 30, 1996)	July 23, 1986
Princess Anne and Timothy Laurence	December 12, 1992
Prince Charles and Camilla Parker Bowles	April 9, 2005
Prince William and Kate Middleton	April 29, 2011

The school day as we knew it: the cane

- The cane was still available to teachers up until 1986, but even by the 1960s it was often only the head who would actually use it.
- If you grew up in Scotland you may have had the tawse, a leather strap, instead.
- Forewarning of a caning meant you could either wear an extra pair of pants or stuff an exercise book down your trousers.
- In some schools a certain number of canings (perhaps three) would lead to suspension from the school.

Mnemonics

The colours of the rainbow
Read over your geography books in vacation or
Richard of York gave battle in vain.
(Red, orange, yellow, green, blue, indigo, violet).

Planets in the solar system
My Very Easy Method: Just Set Up Nine Planets.
(Mercury, Venus, Earth, Mars, Jupiter, Saturn, Uranus, Neptune, Pluto).

Royal houses of England and Great Britain
No Plan Like Yours To Study History Wisely.
(Norman, Plantagenet, Lancaster, York, Tudor, Stuart, Hanover, Windsor).

The seven continents
Eat An Aspirin After A Night-time Snack.
(Europe, Antarctica, Asia, Africa, North America, South America)

The four oceans:
I am a person.
(Indian, Atlantic, Antarctic, Pacific).

Lines of the treble clef
Every good boy deserves fourpence (or favour, or flogging!).
(The musical notes EGBDF).

Spaces of the treble clef
Face.
(The musical notes FACE).

Lines of the bass clef
Every good boy deserves fourpence always.
(The musical notes EGBDFA).

Spaces of the bass clef
All cows eat grass.
(The musical notes ACEG).

Periods of tenure of some British public figures

Archbishop of Canterbury

	Period in office
Geoffrey Fisher	1945-61
Michael Ramsey	1961-74
Donald Coggan	1974-80
Robert Runcie	1980-91
George Carey	1991-2002
Rowan Williams	2003-2012
Justin Welby	2013-

Poet Laureate

	Period in office
John Masefield	1930-67
Cecil Day Lewis	1968-72
John Betjeman	1972-84
Ted Hughes	1984-99
Andrew Motion	1999-2009
Carol Ann Duffy	2009-

General Secretary of the TUC

	Period in post
Vincent Tewson	1946-60
George Woodcock	1960-69
Vic Feather	1969-73
Len Murray	1973-84
Norman Willis	1984-93
John Monks	1993-2003
Brendan Barber	2003-2012

Director-General of the BBC

	Period in post
Sir William Haley	1944-52
Sir Ian Jacob	1952-59
Sir Hugh Greene	1960-69
Sir Charles Curran	1969-77
Sir Ian Trethowan	1977-82
Alasdair Milne	1982-87
Sir Michael Checkland	1987-92
John Birt	1992-2000
Greg Dyke	2000-04
Mark Thompson	2004-2012
George Entwistle	2012
Tim Davie	2012-2013
Tony Hall	2013-

Gents' and ladies' accessories you might remember

Gents: Detachable collars; collar stiffeners; collar studs; tiepins; hair brush; sock suspenders; expandable arm bands; cigarette case; shoe trees; top-pocket handkerchief; monogrammed handkerchiefs; cravat; fob watch; waistcoat; shaving brush; cutthroat razor; leather razor strop; full-length umbrella; steel comb.

Ladies: Hairnets; curlers; hatpins; housecoat; stockings; suspenders; corset; cigarette holder; cotton hanky; smart gloves; fur stole; winged spectacles; headscarf; toque; fake beauty spots; shoulder pads.

Cockney rhyming slang

Adam and Eve = believe
Apples and pears = stairs
Barnet Fair = hair
Bird lime = time
Boat race = face
Borassic lint = skint
Brahms and Liszt = p***ed
Bread and honey = money
Bristol (Bristol City) = titty
Brown bread = dead
Butcher's (hook) = look
China (plate) = mate
Cobblers' awls = balls
Cream crackered = knackered
Daisy roots = boots
Dickie bird = word
Dog and bone = phone

Elephant's trunk = drunk
Frog and toad = road
Hampstead Heath = teeth
Loaf (of bread) = head
Mutton (Mutt and Jeff) = deaf
On your tod (Tod Sloane) = own
Peckham Rye = tie
Pen and ink = stink
Pig's ear = beer
Plates of meat = feet
Rosie Lee – tea
Scarper (Scapa Flow) = go
Syrup (of fig) = wig
Taters (potatoes in the mould) = cold
Trouble and strife = wife
Whistle and flute = suit

Starting dates of factual TV series

1954: *Zoo Quest*

1955: *The Brains Trust; This Is Your Life*

1956: *Zoo Time*

1958: *Grandstand*

1959: *Whicker's World*

1961: *Survival*

1963: *World In Action*

1964: *Horizon; Match Of The Day*

1965: *Man Alive; Tomorrow's World; World of Sport; The Money Programme*

1967: *News At Ten; The World About Us*

1968: *Gardener's World; Sportsnight*

1969: *Nationwide*

1971: *Parkinson*

1972: *Pebble Mill At One*

1973: *That's Life!*

The Dandy

The first issue of *The Dandy Comic* was dated December 4, 1937, priced 2d
and came with a free tinplate whistle. The first issue included:

• Korky The Cat • Desperate Dan • Our Gang • Hungry Horace • Keyhole Kate • Wig And Wam •
• Podge • Bamboo Town • Freddy The Fearless Fly •

Over the next few years the following characters were introduced:

Strip	Year	Strip	Year
Black Bob	1944	Crackaway Twins	1960
Plum McDuff	1948	Dirty Dick	1960
Wuzzy Wiz – Magic is His Biz	1949	Ali Ha-Ha	1960
Sir Solomon Snoozer	1949	Corporal Clott	1960
Rusty	1950	Jammy Mr Sammy	1960
Fighting Forkbeard		Winker Watson	
– The Sea Wolf From Long Ago	1951	– the World's Wiliest Wangler	1961
Willie Willikin's Pobble	1952	Jo White and the 7 Dwarfs	1963
The Streakolight Express	1954	Sunny Boy – He's a Bright Spark	1963
Screwy Driver	1955	Big Head and Thick Head	1963
Lionheart Logans	1955	The Crimson Ball	1963
Tin Lizzie	1955	Brassneck	1964
Just Jimmy	1956	The Red Wrecker	1964
Charlie the Chimp	1957	Greedy Pigg	1965
The Smasher	1957	The Stinging Swarm	1965
Robin Hood	1958	The Umbrella Men	1965
Robinson and His Dog Crusoe	1958	Bully Beef and Chips	1967
Boy With Iron Hands	1959	Greedy Pigg	1967
Around the World In 80 Days	1959	Spunky and his Spider	1968
Mr Mutt	1959	Island of Monsters	1969

Eating out: Lyons Corner House

These large Art Deco-style restaurants were dotted around London
and elsewhere and finally disappeared in 1977.

Sample menu:

First course	Second course	Pudding
Grapefruit cup	Fish mayonnaise, mixed salad	Pear tart
Crème de Legume	Stewed lamb with rice, carrots peas, mashed potato	Stewed prunes
Cold consommé		Chocolate trifle

Traditional book sizes

Name	Imperial (inches)	Metric (mm)
Imperial folio	15½ x 22	390 x 550
Royal folio	12½ x 20	320 x 500
Imperial quarto	11 x 15	280 x 300
Crown folio	10 x 15	250 x 300
Royal quarto	10 x 12½	250 x 320
Medium quarto	9½ x 12	240 x 300
Demy quarto	8¾ x 11¼	220 x 290
Foolscap folio	8½ x 13½	210 x 340
Imperial octavo	7½ x11	190 x 280
Crown quarto	7½ x 10	190 x 250
Foolscap quarto	6¾ x 8½	170 x 210
Royal octavo	6¼ x 10	150 x 250
Medium octavo	6 x 9½	150 x 240
Demy octavo	5 x 8¾	143 x 222
Large crown octavo	5¼ x 8	129 x 198
Crown octavo	5 x 7½	127 x 190
Foolscap octavo	4¼ x 6¾	108 x 171.5
"A" format	4¼ x 6	111 x 175

The books of the Bible

The Old Testament: Genesis (Adam and Eve; Noah and the flood; Abraham, Isaac, Jacob and Joseph and his coat of many colours); Exodus (Moses, leading the Israelites from Egypt; parting of the Red Sea; the Ten Commandments); Leviticus (laws and priestly rituals); Numbers (the Israelites' years in the wilderness); Deuteronomy (Moses dies in sight of the promised land).

The Historical Books: Joshua (Joshua leads the Israelites' conquest of Canaan); Judges (the history of the judges, including Samson, who rule and guide the Israelites); Ruth; 1 Samuel (the Israelites' first kings, Saul and David); 2 Samuel (David's reign); 1 Kings (Solomon succeeds David; the promised land is split into two kingdoms, Israel and Judah; the story of Elijah); 2 Kings; 1 Chronicles (David's reign); 2 Chronicles (Solomon's reign); Ezra; Nehemiah; Esther.

The Poetical Books: Job; Psalms; Proverbs; Ecclesiastes; Song Of Solomon.

The Major Prophets: Isaiah (prophesies doom for kingdom of Judah; prophesies the birth of a child who will save Judah); Jeremiah; Lamentations; Ezekiel; Daniel (Belshazzar's feast, Daniel in the lion's den); Hosea; Joel; Amos; Obadiah; Jonah; Micah; Nahum; Habakkuk; Zephaniah; Haggai; Zechariah; Malachi.

The New Testament: *The Gospels:* Matthew; Mark; Luke; John.

The Early Church: Acts.

Letters of St Paul and Other Letters: Romans; 1 Corinthians; 2 Corinthians; Galatians; Ephesians; Philippians; Colossians; 1 Thessalonians; 2 Thessalonians; 1 Timothy; 2 Timothy; Titus; Philemon; Hebrews; James; 1 Peter; 2 Peter; 1 John; 2 John; 3 John; Jude.

Apocalyptic Prophecy: The Book Of Revelation.

Advertising slogans from our youth: cigarettes, cigars, tobacco & matches

- You're never alone with a Strand. The cigarette of the moment.
- Players, please!
- A man at sea will often hanker/ For the flavour of an Anchor!
- Whatever the pleasure, Players complete it.
- Have a Capstan – they're blended better.
- Wills's Woodbines – smoked by millions.
- More doctors smoke Camels than any other cigarette.
- Consulate – cool as a mountain stream.
- No thank you, I'd rather have a Kensitas!
- The luxury length cigarette! (Ambassador)
- So much satisfaction! (Anchor cigarettes)
- Senior Service satisfy.
- People are changing to Guards.
- Come to where the flavour is. Come to Marlboro Country.
- They've got to be great to be Guards.
- Never go without a Capstan.
- Ah, Woodbine – a great little cigarette.
- I'd walk a mile for a Camel!
- The big cigar for the price of a pint. (Castella cigars)
- Rich, slow-burning Condor – a man's taste!
- Aaah! Condor! It's that Condor moment!
- For men who feel strongly about cigarette taste.
  Ask for Capstan Full Strength in the brown packet.
- Happiness is a cigar called Hamlet
  – the mild cigar from Benson and Hedges.
- Sheer enjoyment from Manikin – Britain's favourite cigar.
- I like a man who smokes St Bruno.
- 3d well spent! (Brymay matches)

Dates in the history of British road travel

1926   First traffic signals introduced in London.
1930   Third party car insurance made compulsory.
1931   The Highway Code introduced.
1934   Belisha beacons introduced (named after Leslie Hore-Belisha, then Minister for Transport); cat's eyes introduced.
1935   Driving tests introduced; 30mph speed limit introduced in urban areas.
1949   First zebra crossings introduced (originally with blue and yellow stripes).
1958   The UK's first parking meter fitted in Grosvenor Square, London.
1960   Traffic wardens introduced in London.
1960   MoT tests introduced for cars more than 10 years old.
1965   Push-button "panda" crossings introduced.
1967   Breathalyzer introduced; MoT necessary for cars over three years old.
1967   All new cars had to have three-point seatbelts in the front seats.
1969   Introduction of the Pelican crossing.
1971   The Green Cross code introduced.
1973   Wearing a crash helmet made compulsory for motorcyclists.
1974   First cars produced fitted with airbags.
1982   It is made an offence not to wear a seatbelt in the front seats.

Royal deaths

King George V	January 20, 1936
King George VI	February 6, 1952
Queen Mary	March 24, 1953
Princess Diana	August 31, 1997
Princess Margaret	February 9, 2002
HM Queen Mother	March 30, 2002

Things you'd be told at the dining table

- Don't speak with your mouth full.
- Keep your elbows off the table.
- Don't leave the table without asking.
- You can't leave the table until your plate is empty.
- You have to eat all your "greens".
- Don't reach across other people for the salt and pepper.
- Sit up straight; don't slouch!

Explanations of old phrases & sayings

As keen as mustard

Meaning:	Very enthusiastic.
Likely origin:	"Keen" also means "sharp", and mustard has a sharpness in flavour, hence the phrase.
Unlikely origin:	An 18th-century mustard manufacturer named Keen – but he didn't begin business until 70 years after the phrase "keen as mustard" appeared in William Walker's *Phraseologia Anglo-Latina* in 1672.

Keep your powder dry

Meaning:	Save your resources for necessary action.
Likely origin:	Oliver Cromwell advised his men while crossing a river with their muskets to "Put your trust in God, but mind to keep your powder dry."
Unlikely origin:	Regency dandies used face powder to improve their looks and strived to keep it dry to avoid it looking patchy.

Keep your nose to the grindstone

Meaning:	Work hard and keep your eye on the job in hand.
Likely origin:	When using grindstones, workers would need to keep a close eye on what they were doing to ensure a good job.
Unlikely origin:	Before plastic surgery was widely available, people with overlarge noses would be encouraged to whittle them down with this primitive method.

Kick the bucket

Meaning:	To die.
Likely origin:	A person committing suicide might have stood on a bucket to hang themselves and then kick it away to complete the job.
Unlikely origin:	When cattle suddenly die in their stalls they keel over and inadvertently kick their feed buckets.

Beyond the pale

Meaning:	Outrageous, beyond the norms of civilized behaviour.
Likely origin:	In ancient times the pale was a wooden stake that was used to denote the boundaries of a settlement. Anyone who went "beyond the pale" was thought to be outside "civilization".
Unlikely origin:	The further north people lived, the colder the weather and hence the whiter their skin. Anyone living beyond the merely pale inhabitants in the furthest reaches of civilization was hopelessly out of touch with mainstream society.

Hat trick

Meaning:	Doing something successfully three times in succession.
Likely origin:	Once upon a time, cricket clubs would give a nice new hat to any player who managed to take three wickets with three consecutive balls.
Unlikely origin:	Shoplifters managing to conceal one hat about their person without detection were commonplace; those who could hide two without getting caught were considered accomplished; people who successfully pinched three hats were hailed as experts.

Cadbury's

John Cadbury first opened a shop in Birmingham in 1824. He set up a company producing cocoa and chocolate in 1831 and this was taken over by his sons Richard and George in 1861.

Dairy Milk: First produced in 1905, it had a higher proportion of milk than other previously available chocolate bars. Cadbury's Fruit and Nut bar followed in 1928 and Whole Nut in 1933.

Flake: Launched in 1920 after a Cadbury's employee noticed how excess chocolate spilled from the moulds while other bars were being produced, forming layers of crumbly, flaky chocolate.

Crème Egg: Cadbury's sold a filled egg from 1923. The Crème Egg as known today was launched in 1963 as Fry's Crème Egg and renamed Cadbury's Crème Egg from 1971.

Crunchie: Originally launched in 1929 by J S Fry, which had merged with Cadbury's in 1919.

Roses: First sold in 1938. The slogan "Say thank you with Roses" was introduced in 1979.

Aztec: The legendary "feast of a bar" (not unlike a Mars Bar) was launched in 1967.

Amazin' Raisin: The Amazin' Raisin bar was launched in 1971, price 5p.

Cadbury's also launched Milk Tray in 1915, Fudge in 1948, Picnic in 1958, Buttons in 1960 and Curly Wurly in 1970.

ITV newsreaders of the 1950s, '60s & '70s

Barbara Mandell • Robert Kee • Gordon Honeycombe • Reginald Bosanquet • Alastair Burnet • Sandy Gall • Andrew Gardner • Leonard Parkin • Michael Nicholson • Peter Sissons • Anna Ford • Trevor MacDonald

Correct forms of address: clergy and judiciary

Anglican clergy:

Archbishop	Archbishop or Your Grace
Bishop	Bishop or My Lord
Dean/Provost	Dean/Provost or Mr Dean/Mr Provost
Chaplain to the armed forces	Padre

Catholic clergy:

The Pope	Your Holiness or Dear Holy Father
Cardinal	Your Eminence

In court:

Judges in higher court	My Lord or My Lady
Circuit judges	Your honour
Lay magistrates	Your worship

List of places that have changed names

Abyssinia – Ethiopia
Ayers Rock – Uluru
Belgian Congo – Democratic Republic of Congo
Biafra – now part of Nigeria
Bombay – Mumbai
Burma – Myanmar
Calcutta – Kolkata
Ceylon – Sri Lanka
Czechoslovakia – Czech Republic and Slovakia
French Guinea – Guinea
French Somaliland – Dijbouti
French Sudan – Mali
Gold Coast – Ghana
Grain Coast – Liberia
Kampuchea – Cambodia
Leningrad – St Petersburg (was Petrograd and then Leningrad)
Madras – Chennai
Northern Rhodesia – Zambia
Peking – Beijing
Persia – Iran
Salisbury (Rhodesia) – Harare
Southern Rhodesia – Zimbabwe
Stalingrad – Volgograd
Yugoslavia – Bosnia, Serbia, Slovenia...
Zaire – Democratic Republic of Congo (Belgian Congo)
Tanganyika – Tanzania

Catchphrases from the age of steam radio

"Before your very eyes!"
Arthur Askey (*Band Waggon*)

"Ay-thang-yaw'll!"
Arthur Askey (*Band Waggon*)

"Hello, playmates!"
Arthur Askey (*Band Waggon*)

"Mind my bike!"
Jack Warner (*Garrison Theatre*)

"Can you hear me, mother?"
Sandy Powell

"Good morning, sir.
Was there something?"
Sam Costa
(*Much Binding In The Marsh*)

"Oh I say! I *am* a fool!"
Maurice Denham
(*Much Binding In The Marsh*)

"Have you read
any good books lately?"
Richard Murdoch
(*Much Binding In The Marsh*)

"Stop it, you saucebox!"
Peter Sellers (*Ray's A Laugh*)

"What's it matter what you
do as long as you tear 'em up?"
Jon Pertwee (*Waterlogged Spa*)

"Are you sitting comfortably?
Then I'll begin."
Julia Lang (*Listen With Mother*)

"Oh, please yourselves!"
Frankie Howerd (*Variety Bandbox*)

"Flippin' kids!"
Tony Hancock (*Educating Archie*)

"Ooh, Ron!"
June Whitfield (*Take It From Here*)

"That's a good idea, son!"
Max Bygraves (*Educating Archie*)

"I've arrived, and to prove it, I'm here!"
Max Bygraves (*Educating Archie*)

"Good evening, each!"
Beryl Reid (*Educating Archie*)

"Stone me; what a life!"
Tony Hancock
(*Hancock's Half Hour*)

"Stop messing about!"
Kenneth Williams
(*Hancock's Half Hour*)

"Left hand down a bit."
Leslie Phillips (*The Navy Lark*)

"Well, I think the answer lies in the soil."
Kenneth Williams (*Beyond Our Ken*)

Instructions for operating an old telephone box

The traditional red telephone box was designed by Giles Gilbert Scott. Officially it was known as the K6, although it was popularly named the Jubilee Box because it was introduced in 1936, the year of King George V's silver jubilee:

Open door (this will be fairly stiff, as door is designed to close if carelessly left open).

A black rotary dial phone is on a stand to your left with a receiver attached to it with a heavy-duty cord.

Next to this is a coin-box with two buttons, A and B.

Four old pennies need to be inserted to make a call before the number is dialled.

When the phone is answered, press button A to release the coins into the machine.

If there is no answer, press button B and your coins will be returned.

Panels on the wall behind the phone provide information on, for example, the numbers to dial for different exchanges, the numbers for emergency calls, advertisements and a mirror in which to check your appearance before leaving the box.

The school day as we knew it: free milk

- The School Milk Act of 1946 ensured that all future wrinklies would be entitled to a third of a pint of milk every day at school until the age of 18.
- Harold Wilson's government scrapped the entitlement for secondary schoolchildren in 1968.
- In 1971 Margaret Thatcher, then Education Minister, ended school milk for over-sevens.
- Some "lucky" children were also given cod liver oil capsules.

Exclamations from the past

Great Scott!	Shut your mush!
That really takes the biscuit!	It's brass monkeys!
You're pulling my leg!	Stone the crows!
Well, I'll go to the foot of our stairs!	Gordon Bennett!
Hell's bells!	Flippin' 'eck!
Stone me!	Blimey O'Reilly!
Gor' blimey!	Blinkin' 'eck
Fiddlesticks!	Pull the other one; it's got bells on it!

Quotes from the Duke of Edinburgh's travels

"If you stay here much longer you'll all be slitty-eyed."

(To British students in China)

"How do you keep the natives off the booze long enough to pass the test?"

(To a Scottish driving instructor)

"Do you still throw spears at each other?"

(To an Australian Aborigine)

"Oh no, I might catch some ghastly disease."

(Upon being asked during a visit to Australia if he would like to stroke a koala – Australia's national symbol)

"We don't come here for our health. We can think of other ways of enjoying ourselves."

(While on a visit to Canada)

"Your country is one of the most notorious centres of trading in endangered species in the world."

(While accepting a conservation award in Thailand)

"And what exotic part of the world do you come from?"

(To Lord Taylor of Warwick, a black member of the House of Lords. Lord Taylor's response: "I'm from Birmingham.")

"So you can write then? Ha, ha!"

(To a 14-year-old boy who had written a letter inviting the royal family to his school)

Starting dates of famous TV comedy series

1955   *I Love Lucy; The Benny Hill Show* (BBC)
1956   *Hancock's Half Hour; The Arthur Haynes Show;*
      The Idiot Weekly Price 2d; A Show Called Fred; Whacko
1957   *The Army Game; The Phil Silvers Show (Sergeant Bilko)*
1958   *The Larkins*
1961   *It's a Square World; Marriage Lines;*
      The Morecambe and Wise Show (ITV); *The Rag Trade*
1962   *Hugh and I; Steptoe and Son; That Was the Week That Was*
1963   *The Dick Van Dyke Show; Meet the Wife*
1964   *The Beverly Hillbillies; The Likely Lads; Not Only But Also*
1965   *The Addams Family; The Munsters; Till Death Us Do Part*
1966   *All Gas and Gaiters; The Frost Report; The Monkees; On the Margin*
1967   *At Last the 1948 Show; Do Not Adjust Your Set;*
      Never Mind the Quality, Feel the Width;
      Not In Front of the Children
1968   *Dad's Army; Father Dear Father; Marty;*
      The Morecambe and Wise Show (BBC); *Nearest and Dearest;*
      Oh, Brother; Please, Sir!
1969   *The Benny Hill Show* (ITV); *Doctor in the House; The Dustbinmen;*
      The Gnomes of Dulwich; Here's Lucy; Joker's Wild; The Liver Birds;
      Me Mammy; Monty Python's Flying Circus;
      On The Buses; Q5; Sez Les; Up Pompeii
1970   *For The Love of Ada; The Lovers; The Goodies*
1971   *And Mother Makes Three; Bless This House; The Comedians;*
      Dave Allen At Large; The Mary Tyler Moore Show; The Two Ronnies
1972   *Love Thy Neighbour*
1973   *Last of the Summer Wine; M*A*S*H; Man About the House;*
      Some Mothers Do 'Ave 'Em; Whatever Happened to The Likely Lads?
1974   *Happy Ever After; It Ain't Half Hot, Mum; Oh No, It's Selwyn Froggitt;*
      Porridge; Rising Damp
1975   *Fawlty Towers; Happy Days*
1976   *The Fall and Rise of Reginald Perrin; George and Mildred;*
      Open All Hours; Yus, My Dear
1977   *Citizen Smith; Mind Your Language*
1978   *The Kenny Everett Video Show*
1979   *Mork and Mindy; Not the Nine O'Clock News; Terry and June*
1981   *Only Fools and Horses*

For US series, starting dates shown are for first broadcast in UK.

Scout and Guide badges

Boy Scouts:

Ambulance, Artist, Athlete, Basket Maker, Boatman, Bookbinder, Camper, Coast Watchman, Climber, Engineer, Entertainer, Explorer, Folk-Dancer, Forester, Interpreter, Journalist, King Scout, Leather Worker, Marksman, Mason, Master-At-Arms, Metal Worker, Miner, Missioner, Naturalist, Oarsman, Piper, Prospector, Public Health Man, Surveyor, Pilot, Plumber, Printer, Reader, Rescuer, Rigger, Sea Fisherman, Signaller, Stalker, Star Man, Swimmer, Tailor, Tracker, Wireless, World Friendship, Weather Man.

Girl Guides:

Ambulance, Athlete, Angler, Aquarist, Artist, Astronomer, Authoress, Backwoodsman, Basket Weaver/Maker/Worker*, Bee Farmer/Keeper*, Bell Ringer, Birdwatcher, Camper, Carpenter/Woodworker*, Collector, Cook, Cyclist, Embroiderer/Embroideress*, First Aid, Friend To Animals, Gardener, Gymnast, Hiker, Homemaker, Horsewoman, Knitter, Knotter, Landgirl, Lifesaver, Mapreader, Needlewoman, Pathfinder, Signaller, Swimmer, Woodman.

Some badge names changed over the years, as shown.

Lessons you used to be told

- Children should be seen and not heard.
- Always offer your seat to older people on the bus/train, etc.
- Always say "please" and "thank you".
- Don't take sweets from strangers.
- Put your hand over your mouth when you cough/yawn.
- Pick your feet up when you walk.
- Don't speak until you're spoken to.

Idiomatic phrases

A nod's as good as a wink
All fingers and thumbs
    (should be "all fingers are thumbs")
Another string to your bow
As sure as eggs is eggs
At sixes and sevens
At the end of one's tether
Beer and skittles
Before you can say Jack Robinson
Between you, me and the bedpost
Born with a silver spoon in one's mouth
By the skin of one's teeth
Can't see the wood for the trees
Chip off the old block
Chip on one's shoulder
Clip one's wings
Cooked his goose
Cut off your nose to spite your face
Dead as a dodo
Don't beat about the bush
Don't look a gift horse in the mouth
Drive a coach and four through
Dutch courage
Eating humble pie
Elbow grease
From pillar to post
Full of beans
Going against the grain
Got out of the wrong side of the bed
Hauled over the coals
Having an axe to grind
He's been burning the candle at both ends
Hit the nail on the head
Hoist with one's own petard
I've a bone to pick with you
Keep the wolf from the door
Keeping body and soul together
Keeping up with the Joneses
Knock into a cocked hat
Knows which side his bread is buttered
Laughing on the other side of your face

Let the cat out of the bag
Let them stew in their own juice
Let's bury the hatchet
Lick into shape
Make both ends meet
Make mincemeat of
Nail one's colours to the mast
Neither rhyme nor reason
New brooms sweep clean
Not by a long chalk
Not in a month of Sundays
Not worth the candle
On the horns of a dilemma
Pig in a poke
Plain as a pikestaff
Pot calling the kettle black
Raining cats and dogs
Red letter day
Ringing the changes
Robbing Peter to pay Paul
Run the gauntlet
See how the land lies
Show a clean pair of heels
Skeleton in the cupboard
Snuffed out
Spick and span
Splice the mainbrace
Sprat to catch a mackerel
Square peg in a round hole
Storm in a teacup
Take a leaf out of (someone's) book
Tarred with the same brush
The fat is in the fire
Three sheets to the wind
Throw down the gauntlet
Tied to mother's apron strings
Tip the wink
To wet one's whistle
Take the gilt off the gingerbread
Turn over a new leaf
When my ship comes in

Dinky and Corgi cars

Meccano began producing Dinky Toys cars in Liverpool in 1934.
The first six models were:
22a Sports Car • 22b Sports Coupe • 22c Motor Truck
22d Delivery Van • 22e Tractor • 22f Tank

Corgi Toys were produced in Swansea and first appeared in 1956.
Corgi's first models were: Ford Consul (200/200M) • Austin A50 Cambridge
(201/201M) • Morris Cowley (202/202M) • Vauxhall Velox (203/203M)•
Rover 90 (204/204M) • Riley Pathfinder (205/205M) • Hillman Husky
(206/206M) • Austin-Healey 100 (300) • Triumph TR2 (301) •

Dinky and Corgi TV and film tie-in models:

Model	Vehicle	Year issued	TV series/ Film	
258	The Saint's Volvo P1800	1965	*The Saint*	Corgi
261	James Bond's Aston Martin DB5	1965	*Goldfinger*	Corgi
497	Man From Uncle THRUSH-buster Car	1966	*The Man From UNCLE*	Corgi
267	The Batmobile	1966	*Batman*	Corgi
GS7	Daktari Gift Set	1966	*Daktari*	Corgi
100	Lady Penelope's FAB1	1967	*Thunderbirds*	Dinky
101	Thunderbird 2	1967	*Thunderbirds*	Dinky
106	Mini Moke	1967	*The Prisoner*	Dinky
103	Spectrum Patrol Car	1968	*Captain Scarlet*	Dinky
104	Spectrum Pursuit Vehicle	1968	*Captain Scarlet*	Dinky
266	Chitty Chitty Bang Bang	1968	*Chitty Chitty Bang Bang*	Corgi
277	The Monkeemobile	1968	*The Monkees*	Corgi
102	Joe's Car	1969	*Joe 90*	Dinky
802	Popeye's Paddle Wagon	1969	*Popeye*	Corgi
803	The Beatles Yellow Submarine	1969	*Yellow Submarine*	Corgi
351	Interceptor	1971	*UFO*	Dinky
352	Ed Straker's Car	1971	*UFO*	Dinky
354	The Pink Panther's Car	1972	*The Pink Panther*	Dinky

Britain's first stretches of motorway

When opened	Name	Location	Length	Other info
December 1958	M6 Preston by-pass	Preston, Lancashire	8.25 miles	Opened by Prime Minister Harold Macmillan
September 1959	M4 Chiswick Flyover	Chiswick, Greater London	0.5 miles	Not actually part of the motorway when built
November 1959	M1 Crick to Berrygrove section	Crick, Northants to Berrygrove, Watford	67 miles	The first full inter-city motorway
April 1960	M6 Lancaster by-pass	East of Lancaster, connecting with A6	11.5 miles	Has 27 bridges
October 1960	M63 Stretford/ Eccles by-pass	South west of Stretford and Eccles	5 miles	Now part of M60
November 1960	M50 Ross Spur	North of Ross-on-Wye	22 miles	Building started in March 1958 before the M6 Preston by-pass was built

Great British toy manufacturers

Company	Location	Well Known Products
Meccano	Binns Road, Liverpool	Meccano construction sets
Hornby	Binns Road, Liverpool	Hornby Dublo model railways
Chad Valley	Harborne, Birmingham	Soft toys, puzzles, board games etc. *(near the Chad stream!)*
Lesney Products	Hackney, London	Matchbox cars
Palitoy	Coalville, Leicestershire	Action Man, Pippa dolls, Tiny Tears
Tri-ang	Margate, Kent	Model trains, cars, Skalextric
Pelham Puppets	Marlborough, Wiltshire	String, glove and rod puppets
Denys Fisher	Leeds, West Yorkshire	Spirograph, Stickle Bricks, Etch-a-Sketch

Enid Blyton mystery book series

THE SECRET SERIES
(Five books; 1938-53)

Mike Arnold
Peggy Arnold
Nora Arnold
Jack (the friend the Arnolds make after moving to
      the country to live with their aunt and uncle)

The Secret Island,
The Secret of Spiggy Holes,
The Secret Mountain,
The Secret of Killimooin etc

THE ADVENTUROUS FOUR
(Two books; 1941-47)

Jill (Mary's twin sister)
Mary (Jill's twin sister)
Tom (Jill and Mary's brother)
Andy (a fisher boy whom they befriend
      while on holiday in Scotland)

The Adventurous Four
The Adventurous Four Again

THE FAMOUS FIVE
(21 books; 1942-62)

Julian Kirrin
Dick Kirrin (Julian's younger brother)
Anne Kirrin (Julian and Dick's younger sister)
George Kirrin (aka Georgina, their tomboy cousin)
Timmy (George's dog)

Five On a Treasure Island,
Five Run Away Together,
Five Go to Smuggler's Top,
Five Go to Billycock Hill etc

THE FIVE FINDER-OUTERS
(15 books; 1943-61)

Fatty (Frederick Algernon Trotteville)
Larry Daykin
Daisy Daykin (Larry's younger sister)
Pip Hilton
Bets Hilton (Pip's younger sister)
Buster (Fatty's Scottish terrier)

The Mystery of the Burnt Cottage,
The Mystery of the Disappearing Cat,
The Mystery of the Spiteful Letters etc

THE ADVENTURE SERIES
(Eight books; 1944-55)

Philip Mannering
Jack Trent
Dinah Mannering (Philip's younger sister)
Lucy-Ann Trent (Jack's younger sister)
Kiki (Jack's pet cockatoo)

The Island of Adventure,
The Castle of Adventure,
The Sea of Adventure,
The Mountain of Adventure etc

THE SECRET SEVEN
(15 books; 1949-63)

Peter (leader of the Secret Seven)
Janet (Peter's sister)
Jack (Peter's best friend)
Pam (a girl from Janet's school)
Barbara (Pam's best friend)
Colin (a boy from Peter's school)
George (Colin's best friend)
Scamper (Janet and Peter's dog)

The Secret Seven,
Secret Seven on the Trail,
Go Ahead Secret Seven,
Good Work Secret Seven etc

THE BARNEY MYSTERIES
(6 books; 1949-59)

Roger Lynton
Diana Lynton (Roger's sister)
Snubby (their cousin)
Barney (a boy circus worker)
Miranda (Barney's pet monkey)

The Rockingdown Mystery,
The Rilloby Fair Mystery,
The Ring O'Bells Mystery,
The Rubadub Mystery etc

Mars

Mars Incorporated was founded by Frank C and Ethel V Mars in Minneapolis. Their son Forrest Mars established Mars Limited in the UK in Slough in 1932. Their products have included:

Mars Bar: The nougat and caramel chocolate coated bar first produced by Mars in Slough in 1932. It was a sweeter version of the bar sold by Mars in the US and known as Milky Way. The Milky Way introduced in Britain was a different bar with a lighter whipped centre and no caramel. In the 1930s, a Mars Bar cost 2d.

Maltesers: Developed in 1936 by Forrest Marrs and originally sold as Energy Balls.

Twix: First produced in the UK in 1967.

Iconic trains: the Mallard

- Designed, like the *Flying Scotsman*, by Sir Nigel Gresley.
- Set a world record speed (125.88mph) for a steam locomotive.
- Ran on the East Coast main line.
- Finally went into the sidings for the last time in 1963.

PE exercises

Bean bags   Catching; balancing on head; juggling; throwing into hula hoop placed on floor.

Hula hoops   Swinging round hips; throwing over another person who had to stand absolutely still in a human game of hoopla; jumping in and out of hula hoops placed on floor.

Star jumps   Jumping up and down, and extending arms and legs sideways to make a star shape.

Earliest characters in *The Archers*

The Archers was first broadcast on May 29, 1950, as a Midlands regional programme entitled *The Archers Of Wimberton Farm*.

The series went national with *Announcing The Archers*, broadcast in December 1950, and the first episode proper aired on January 1, 1951.

Early characters included:

Dan Archer *(owner of Brookfield Farm in Ambridge, Borsetshire)*

Doris Archer *(Dan's wife).*

Jack Archer *(Phil's older brother, the manager of the Bull public house).*

Peggy Archer *(Jack's wife, later Peggy Woolley, gave birth to Tony Archer shortly after the series started in February 1951).*

Mrs P *(Mrs Perkins, Peggy's mother, who moved to Ambridge following Tony's birth).*

Walter Gabriel *(an ageing smallholder and friend of the Archers; known for saying: "My old pal, my old beauty...").*

Phil Archer *(Dan and Doris' son).*

Grace Fairbrother *(the daughter of Phil's employer, later to be Phil's wife).*

Jane Maxwell *(a willowy blonde to whom Phil was attracted and to whom he gave a job looking after Fairbrother's poultry scheme).*

Lieutenant Alan Carey *(a veteran of the war in Korea to whom Grace was attracted).*

Christine Archer *(Dan and Doris' daughter).*

Dick Raymond *(a reporter on the Borsetshire Echo, Christine's boyfriend).*

Basil Grove *(a character with whom Christine had a love affair).*

Keith Latimer *(a mineralogist who was brought in to perform test drillings for ironstone on Fairbrother's land and who became friendly with Christine – who didn't?!).*

Bill Slater *(a Londoner and asthma sufferer who was given a job at Brookfield but found to be a bad worker, died following a fight outside the Bull, and was later discovered to have been sabotaging Latimer's diamond drill bit).*

Advertising slogans from our youth: tea, coffee and milk drinks

- Join the tea set. (Ty-Phoo).
- Everyone drinks Ty-Phoo!
- Ty-Phoo puts the "T" in Britain. The "T" that stands for taste!
- For the tea that picks you up, pick up Ty-Phoo!
- Tetley make tea bags make tea.
- A cup of D (Brooke Bond Dividend).
- The drink that's as warm as mink (Cadbury's Drinking Chocolate).
- Cup hands, here comes Cadbury's (Cadbury's Drinking Chocolate).
- Horlicks guards against night starvation.
- Look into the jar, it's a deep rich brown, 'cause there's coffee pot freshness all the way down! (Maxwell House).
- We are the Ovaltineys, happy girls and boys/Make your request; we'll not refuse you/We are here just to amuse you/Would you like a song or story, will you share our joys?/ At games and sports we're more than keen; No merrier children could be seen/Because we all drink Ovaltine, We're happy girls and boys!
- Drink Ovaltine! Help put back what winter takes out of you! Ovaltine – good for athletes, good for you.
- All the family love Carnation, because it's double rich, all the family love Carnation.
- Drinka pinta milka day. (Dairy Council).
- Drink a glass of Nesquik! Nesquik's fun!
- Watch out, there's a Humphrey about. (Unigate).
- It's the little perforations that make all the difference. (Tetley's tea).
- Mellow Birds will make you smile!
- Make every day good to the last drop. (Maxwell House).
- America's favourite coffee. (Maxwell House).
- Auntie Sue pours any old brew, and dear Aunt Jane pours out pure rain, but mother sees we've Co-op Teas!
- Avez-vous un cuppa? (PG Tips).
- Dad, do you know the piano's on my foot? (PG Tips).

Dates in British history

October 14, 1066: Battle of Hastings.
December 25, 1066: Coronation of William the Conqueror.
December 19, 1154: Coronation of Henry II.
December 29, 1170: Murder of Thomas à Becket.
October 12, 1189: Richard the Lionheart leaves England for the Crusades.
June 20, 1214: Oxford University chartered.
June 15, 1215: Signing of Magna Carta.
January 20, 1265: First English Parliament held
May 24, 1337: Beginning of the Hundred Years War.
August 26, 1346: Battle of Crécy.
June 15, 1381: End of the Peasants' Revolt.
July 21, 1403: Battle of Shrewsbury.
October 25, 1415: Battle of Agincourt.
August 22, 1485: Battle of Bosworth.
April 21, 1509: Death of Henry VII and accession of Henry VIII.
July 6, 1535: Execution of Thomas More.
May 19, 1536: Execution of Anne Boleyn.
July 19, 1545: Sinking of the *Mary Rose*.
January 28, 1547: Death of Henry VIII and accession of Edward VI.
March 21, 1556: Thomas Cranmer burnt at the stake.
January 15, 1559: Elizabeth I crowned.
April 23, 1564: Birth of William Shakespeare.
September 26, 1580: Francis Drake completes the first circumnavigation of the globe.
February 8, 1587: Execution of Mary, Queen of Scots.
July 29, 1588: Defeat of the Spanish Armada.
December 31, 1600: East India Company chartered.
March 24, 1603: Death of Elizabeth I.
November 5, 1605: The Gunpowder Plot.
April 12, 1606: The Union Jack created.
May 2, 1611: The King James Bible published.
December 21, 1620: The Pilgrim Fathers land in Massachusetts.
August 22, 1642: Beginning of the English Civil War.
January 30, 1649: Execution of Charles I.
December 16, 1653: Oliver Cromwell becomes Lord Protector.
May 25, 1660: The restoration of the monarchy follows Charles II's return to Britain.
September 2, 1666: Great Fire of London starts.
February 13, 1689: William and Mary are proclaimed joint sovereigns.
January 1, 1707: The Act of Union.
October 23, 1707: First Parliament of Great Britain.
April 7, 1739: Dick Turpin hanged at York.
April 16, 1746: Battle of Culloden.
April 29, 1770: Captain James Cook lands in Australia.
December 16, 1773: The "Boston Tea Party".
July 4, 1776: American colonies declare independence.
December 7, 1783: William Pitt becomes youngest PM.
April 28, 1789: Mutiny on the Bounty.
February 1, 1793: Beginning of Napoleonic Wars.

Dates in British history continued

August 1, 1798: Battle of the Nile.
January 9, 1799: Introduction of income tax by William Pitt.
October 21, 1805: Battle of Trafalgar.
July 25, 1814: The steam locomotive demonstrated by George Stephenson.
June 18, 1815: Battle of Waterloo.
August 16, 1819: Peterloo Massacre.
May 5, 1821: Death of Napoleon on St Helena.
June 7, 1832: The Great Reform Act passed.
August 1, 1834: Abolition of slavery in Great Britain and its possessions.
June 20, 1837: Death of William IV and accession of Victoria.
January 10, 1840: Penny post service begins.
May 1, 1851: Great Exhibition opens.
October 25, 1854: Charge of the Light Brigade.
March 30, 1856: Crimean War ends.
May 10, 1857: Indian Mutiny breaks out.
June 9, 1870: Death of Charles Dickens.
November 10, 1871: Dr Livingstone found by Stanley.
March 16, 1872: First FA Cup final.
August 25, 1875: Captain Webb swims the Channel.
January 1, 1877: Victoria is proclaimed Empress of India.
August to November 1888: The Jack the Ripper killings.
October 11, 1899: Beginning of Boer War.
January 22, 1901: Death of Queen Victoria and accession of Edward VII.
March 29, 1912: Death of Captain Robert Falcon Scott.
April 15, 1912: Titanic sinks.
August 4, 1914: Britain declares War on Germany.
July 1, 1916: First Day on the Somme.
July 31, 1917: Third Battle of Ypres.
February 6, 1918: Women get the vote.
April 1, 1918: RAF created from amalgamation of Royal Flying Corps and Royal Naval Air Service.
November 11, 1918: End of the First World War.
October 18, 1922: BBC founded.
December 11, 1936: Abdication of Edward VIII.
September 30, 1938: "Peace in our time" proclaimed by Neville Chamberlain.
September 3, 1939: WW2 begins with declaration of war on Germany.
January 8, 1940: Food rationing introduced.
May 10, 1940: Winston Churchill becomes Prime Minister.
May 27, 1940: Dunkirk evacuation begins.
July 10, 1940: The Battle of Britain begins.
September 7, 1940: Beginning of the Blitz.
October 23, 1942: Battle of El Alamein.
May 16, 1943: The Dambusters raid.
March 24, 1944: The Great Escape.
June 6, 1944: The D-Day landings.
May 7, 1945: Surrender of Nazi Germany. VE Day.
September 2, 1945: Japan signs surrender.
January 25, 1965: Death of Winston Churchill.

The historic counties of England

Bedfordshire • Hampshire • **Oxfordshire** • Berkshire • Herefordshire
Rutlandshire • Buckinghamshire • **Hert**fordshire • Shropshire (Salop)
Cambridgeshire • Huntingdonshire • **Staffordshire** • Cheshire • Kent
Somersetshire • Cornwall (Kernow) • Lancashire • Suffolk • Cumberland
Leicestershire • Surrey • Derbyshire • Lincolnshire • Sussex • Devonshire
Middlesex • Warwickshire • Dorsetshire • Norfolk • Westmorland
Durham • Northamptonshire • Wiltshire • Essex • Northumberland
Worcestershire • Gloucestershire • Nottinghamshire • Yorkshire

The historic counties of Wales

Anglesey (Sir Fôn) • Denbighshire (Sir Ddinbych) • Monmouthshire (Sir Fynwy)
Brecknockshire (Sir Frycheiniog) • Flintshire (Sir y Fflint)
Montgomeryshire (Sir Drefaldwyn) • Caernarfonshire (Sir Gaernarfon)
Glamorganshire (Sir Forgannwg or Morgannwg)
Pembrokeshire (Sir Benfro) • Cardiganshire (Sir Aberteifi or Ceredigion)
Merionethshire (Sir Feirionnydd or Meirionnydd)
Radnorshire (Sir Faesyfed) • Carmarthenshire (Sir Gaerfyrddin or Sir Gâr)

The historic counties of Scotland

Aberdeenshire • Dunbartonshire • Peeblesshire • Angus (until 1928, Forfarshire)
East Lothian (until 1921, Haddingtonshire) • Perthshire • Argyll • Fife
Renfrewshire • Ayrshire • Inverness-shire • Ross and Cromarty • Banffshire
Kincardineshire • Roxburghshire • Berwickshire • Kinross-shire • Selkirkshire
Caithness • Kirkcudbrightshire • Stirlingshire • Clackmannanshire
Lanarkshire • Sutherland • County of Bute
Midlothian (until 1890, County of Edinburgh)
West Lothian (until 1924, Linlithgowshire)
County of Moray (until 1918, also known as Elginshire)
Nairnshire • Wigtownshire • Dumfriesshire
Orkney • Zetland (Shetland)

How to wrap a parcel with brown paper

Step one   Carefully cut the paper to size for the item to be wrapped.

Step two   Fold the paper around the item, fold the top of each end down,
fold the sides of each end in, and fold the bottom of each end (which should now have formed a point) up over the top and side ends.

Step three   Wrap the string around the parcel from end to end so that it holds the pointed ends of the paper in place.
Cross the two ends of the string over the bottom of the parcel and bring them round to the top and tie a double knot.
If desired, a bow can be formed with the string.

Step four   Put a piece of sealing wax on to a spoon and heat gently over a flame.
Once the wax has melted, pour over the string knot.

Step five (optional) To make an impression (literally, as well as metaphorically) press your seal into the wax while it is still soft.

The BBC Green Book

In 1949 the BBC issued a booklet entitled *BBC Variety Programmes Policy Guide For Writers and Producers*. These guidelines became known as the Green Book and were designed to tell writers and producers of BBC comedy programmes which sorts of jokes would not be tolerated.

Good taste and decency were, according to the guide, the obvious governing considerations. It decreed that programmes must "at all cost be kept free of crudities, coarseness and innuendo".

The use of "expletives and forceful language" had "no place at all in light entertainment" and could only be justified "in a serious dramatic setting where the action of the play demands them".

The guide decreed that "All such words as God, Good God, My God, Blast, Hell, Damn, Bloody, Gorblimey, Ruddy, etc etc should be deleted from scripts and innocuous expressions substituted".

"Cleaned up" versions of well-known vulgar jokes (eg the Brass Monkey) were not normally admissible "since the humour in such cases is invariably evident only if the vulgar version is known", and an absolute ban was placed on the following:

Jokes about lavatories, effeminacy in men or immorality of any kind.

References to honeymoon couples, chambermaids, fig leaves, prostitution, ladies' underwear (eg "Winter draws on"), the habits of animals (eg rabbits), lodgers or commercial travellers.

U and Non-U English

The terms "U" and "Non U" were first used in 1954 in a paper on "Upper-Class English Usage" by Professor Alan Ross. They were then popularized by author Nancy Mitford, sister of Jessica, Pamela, Deborah (the Duchess of Devonshire), Diana (Mrs Oswald Mosley) and Unity (once a close friend of Adolf Hitler). "U" stood for upper-class and those who spoke "non-U" immediately marked themselves out as lower- or middle-class. Ross pointed out certain sorts of "U" pronunciation such as:

Word	U Pronunciation	Word	U Pronunciation
Get	Git	Golf	Gofe
Just	Jest	Either	I-ther
Catch	Ketch	Forehead	Forrid
Ralph	Rafe	Handkerchief	Handkerchiff
Hotel	Otel	Tyre	Tar

Certain vocabulary also belonged to "U" or "Non-U":

Non-U	U	Non-U	U
Cemetery	Graveyard	Notepaper	Writing-paper
Cheers	Good health	Pass on	Die
Cycle	Bike or bicycle	Perfume	Scent
Dentures	False teeth	Pleased to meet you	How d'you do?
Dinner	Lunch	Preserve	Jam
Dress suit	Dinner jacket	Radio	Wireless
Glasses	Spectacles	Serviette	Table napkin
Greens	Vegetables	Settee/Couch	Sofa
I was ill on the boat.	I was sick on the boat.	Sick (in bed)	Ill (in bed)
Jack (cards)	Knave	Sweet	Pudding
Lounge	Drawing-room	Teacher	(School) master, mistress
Mantelpiece	Chimneypiece	They have (got) a lovely home.	They've a very nice house.
Mental	Mad	Toilet	Lavatory or loo
Mirror	Looking-glass	Wealthy	Rich

Ross also noted that the word "Pardon?" was used by non-U speakers:
a. if they did not hear a speaker properly; b. as an apology; or
c. after hiccuping or belching. U speakers, on the other hand,
would respond to these situations with
a. What?; b. Sorry; or c. Silence.

UK Toy Retailers' Association most popular toys of the 1950s

1950   Flying Saucer (from Cascelloid's toy division Palitoy).
        Spears' Electric Contact Quiz (when the correct answer is given the electric connection is made and a light comes on).

1951   Selcol Talking Humpty Dumpty with a crank-handle on his side.
        Kiddicraft's "Sensible" range of cot and pram toys.

1952   Pedigree's black baby dolls Mary Lou and Dixie.
        Angela "the doll with magic flesh", sleeping eyes and lashes.
        Wembley (the football board game).
        Waddingtons' Keywords (not unlike Scrabble).

1953   Atom Bomber (toy plane with automatic-release metal A-bombs!)
        The Slinky.

1954   Dan Dare Rota Spinner.
        Spears' Scrabble.

1955   Waddingtons' Scoop (newspaper-based board game).

1956   Bleep Bleep satellite toy (inspired by the launch of Sputnik).

1957   Davy Crockett hats and toys (the Disney live action TV series and film).

1958   The Hula Hoop (20 million sales in its first year).
        Scalextric.
        The Frisbee.

1959   Frido playballs (endorsed by Stanley Matthews).
        Scammell breakdown truck from Matchbox.

Numbers of cars on British roads

1904	28,000
1934	1,500,000
1939	2,000,000
1959	5,000,000
1961	10,000,000
1970	15,000,000
1983	20,000,000
2010	31,000,000

Street games

Hopscotch

Chalk the playing area on to the pavement with boxes numbered one to ten.
Box one has boxes two and three above it followed by box four above them,
and so in singles and pairs with a single box ten at the top. Throw a stone on
to square one and jump on to squares two and three and hop on to square four,
alternately hopping and jumping to square ten. Turn and come back, picking up
your stone on the way. Players take turns and the first to complete the course
having thrown and collected their stone on and from all squares is the winner.

Knock Down Ginger

Knock on people's doors and run away! Simple as that!

British Bulldog

One or two players are picked as bulldogs and all the rest of the players have to
run from one end of the playing area to the other without being caught by the
bulldogs. When they are caught they too become bulldogs. The winner is the
last player to avoid becoming a bulldog.

Tin Can Tommy

A tin can or ball is kicked down the road by one of the players. The person who
has been picked as "it" has to walk down the road and retrieve the can or ball
and walk backwards with it to the starting point. In the meantime the rest of
the players hide. The person who is "it" then has to find them.

BBC weather forecasters

George Cowling (the BBC's first weatherman) • Tom Clifton
• Philip McAllen John Parry • David Dean • Jack Armstrong
Trevor Davies • Bill Bruce • Bert Foord • Jack Scott

Real and stage names of celebrities

Julie Andrews (Julia Elizabeth Wells)
Fred Astaire (Frederick Austerlitz)
Lauren Bacall (Betty Joan Perske)
Anne Bancroft (Anna-Maria Louisa Italiano)
Tony Bennett
(Anthony Dominick Benedetto)
Jack Benny (Benjamin Kubelsky)
Marlon Brando (Marlon Junior Brandeau)
Yul Brynner (Yul Taidje Kahn, Jr.)
George Burns (Nathan Birnbaum)
Richard Burton (Richard Walter Jenkins)
Michael Caine (Maurice Micklewhite)
Cher (Cherilyn Sarkisian)
Joan Crawford (Lucille Le Sueur)
Michael Crawford (Michael Dumble-Smith)
Bing Crosby (Harry Lillis Crosby)
Tony Curtis (Bernard Schwartz)
John Denver (Henry John Deutschendorf Jr.)
Robert Donat (Friedrich Robert Donath)
Kirk Douglas (Issur Danielovitch)
WC Fields (William Claude Dukenfield)
Greta Garbo (Greta Gustafsson)
Judy Garland (Frances Gumm)
Rex Harrison (Reginald Carey)
Rita Hayworth (Margarita Cansino)
Charlton Heston (John Charles Carter)
Bob Hope (Leslie Townes Hope)
Leslie Howard (Leslie Stainer)
Harry Houdini (Ehrich Weiss)
Rock Hudson (Roy Scherer Jr)
Burl Ives (Burle Icle Ivanhoe)
Al Jolson (Asa Yoelson)
Frankie Laine (Frankie LoVecchio)
Veronica Lake
(Constance Frances Marie Ockelman)
Dorothy Lamour (Mary Kaumeyer)
Hedy Lamarr (Hedwig Eva Maria Kiesler)
Mario Lanza (Alfredo Cocozza)
Stan Laurel (Arthur Stanley Jefferson)
Bruce Lee (Lee Jun-Fan)

Peggy Lee (Norma Deloris Egstrom)
Janet Leigh (Jeanette Helen Morrison)
Vivien Leigh (Vivian Mary Hartley)
Jerry Lewis (Joseph Levitch)
Liberace (Wladziu Valentino Liberace)
Sophia Loren (Sofia Villani Scicolone)
Shirley MacLaine (Shirley Beatty)
Jayne Mansfield (Vera Jayne Palmer)
Dean Martin (Dino Paul Crocetti)
Walter Matthau (Walter
Matuschanskayasky)
Marilyn Monroe (Norma Jeane Mortenson,
raised as Norma Jeane Baker)
Maureen O'Hara (Maureen Fitzsimons)
Edith Piaf (Edith Gassion)
Mary Pickford (Gladys Marie Smith)
Anthony Quinn
(Antonio Rudolfo Oaxaca Quinn)
Debbie Reynolds (Mary Frances Reynolds)
Edward G. Robinson
(Emmanuel Goldenberg)
Ginger Rogers (Virginia McMath)
Roy Rogers (Leonard Slye)
Mickey Rooney (Joe Yule Jr.)
Telly Savalas (Aristotelis Harris Savalas)
Jane Seymour (Joyce Frankenberg)
Omar Sharif (Michael Shalhoub)
Barbara Stanwyck (Ruby Stevens)
Connie Stevens (Concetta Ingolia)
Twiggy (Lesley Hornby)
Rudolph Valentino
(Rudolpho D'Antonguolla)
John Wayne (Marion Robert Morrison)
Johnny Weissmuller
(Peter Jànos Weissmuller)
Raquel Welch (Jo Raquel Tejada)
Gene Wilder (Jerome Silberman)
Shelley Winters (Shirley Schrift)
Natalie Wood (Natalia Zakharenko)

Christmas Number One records

1952 Al Martino; *"Here in My Heart"*.
1953 Frankie Laine: *"Answer Me"*.
1954 Winifred Atwell: *"Let's Have Another Party"*.
1955 Dickie Valentine: *"Christmas Alphabet"*.
1956 Johnnie Ray: *"Just Walkin' in the Rain"*.
1957 Harry Belafonte: *"Mary's Boy Child"*.
1958 Conway Twitty: *"It's Only Make Believe"*.
1959 Emile Ford & The Checkmates: *"What Do You Want to Make Those Eyes at Me For?"*
1960 Cliff Richard and The Shadows: *"I Love You"*.
1961 Danny Williams: *"Moon River"*.
1962 Elvis Presley: *"Return to Sender"*.
1963 The Beatles: *"I Want to Hold Your Hand"*.
1964 The Beatles: *"I Feel Fine"*.
1965 The Beatles: *"Day Tripper"* / *"We Can Work it Out"*.
1966 Tom Jones: *"Green, Green Grass of Home"*.
1967 The Beatles: *"Hello, Goodbye"*.
1968 The Scaffold: *"Lily the Pink"*.
1969 Rolf Harris: *"Two Little Boys"*.
1970 Dave Edmunds: *"I Hear You Knocking"*.
1971 Benny Hill: *"Ernie (The Fastest Milkman in the West)"*.
1972 Jimmy Osmond: *"Long Haired Lover From Liverpool"*.
1973 Slade: *"Merry Xmas Everybody"*.
1974 Mud: *"Lonely This Christmas"*.
1975 Queen: *"Bohemian Rhapsody"*.
1976 Johnny Mathis: *"When a Child is Born"*.
1977 Wings: *"Mull of Kintyre"*.
1978 Boney M: *"Mary's Boy Child"* / *"Oh My Lord"*.
1979 Pink Floyd: *"Another Brick in the Wall (Part 2)"*.

How to spot a spiv

- Flashy suit.
- Loud tie.
- Pencil moustache.
- Fedora hat at a jaunty angle.
- Will attempt to relieve you of your money and/or possessions.

Home medical remedies

Condition	Treatment
Whooping cough	Heat tar in the bedroom.
Coughs	Onion juice.
Sore throat	Gargle vinegar and salt water.
Sticky eye	Poultice of used tea leaves.
Chilblains	Soak in urine from the chamber pot.
Diptheria	Isolation.
Scarlet fever	Isolation.

To prevent contagion spreading, hang a blanket soaked in carbolic disinfectant over the bedroom door in which the infected person is lying.

Operating dates of Butlin's holiday camps

Skegness (1936-present)
Filey (1945-83)
Pwllheli (1947)
Bognor Regis (1960-present)
Barry Island (1966-86)

Clacton (1938-83)
Ayr (1947-98)
Mosney, Ireland (1948-80)
Minehead (1962-present)

People who chose their own records when they were guests on Desert Island Discs

Cilla Black (1964) – 1
Engelbert Humperdinck (2004) – 1
Rolf Harris (1999) – 3
Norman Wisdom (2000) – 5
Elisabeth Schwarzkopf (opera singer, 1958) – 7!

Main characters from
Watch With Mother programmes

Programme	First broadcast	Main characters included:
Andy Pandy	1950	Andy Pandy, Teddy, Looby Loo.
The Flowerpot Men	1952	Bill, Ben, Little Weed.
Rag, Tag and Bobtail	1953	Rag (the hedgehog), Tag (the mouse) and Bobtail (the rabbit).
Picture Book	1955	Bizzy Lizzy, the Jolly Jack Tars (the Captain, Mr. Mate, Jonathan the deck hand and Ticky the monkey), Sausage the marionette dachshund.
The Woodentops	1955	Daddy, Mummy, Jenny, Willy, Baby and "the very biggest Spotty Dog you ever did see".
Tales of the Riverbank	1960	Hammy Hamster, Roderick the Water Rat, G.P. the Guinea Pig.
Camberwick Green	1966	Windy Miller, Mrs Honeyman, Doctor Mopp, Captain Snort, Sergeant Major Grout and the soldier boys from Pippin Fort, Mickey Murphy the Baker, PC McGarry No. 452, Farmer Jonathan Bell etc.
The Pogles/ Pogles' Wood	1965	Mr and Mrs Pogle, Pippin and Tog.
Bizzy Lizzy	1967	Bizzy Lizzy, her Eskimo doll Little Mo.
Trumpton	1967	The Mayor, Mr Troop the town clerk, Chippy Minton and his son Nibbs, Captain Flack and the Fire Brigade (Pugh, Pugh, Barney McGrew, Cuthbert, Dibble and Grubb) etc.
Chigley	1969	Lord Belborough, his butler Brackett, Mr Cresswell (owner of the biscuit factory), Mr Swallow of Treddle's Wharf, Harry Farthing the potter and his daughter Winnie etc.
Mary, Mungo and Midge	1969	Mary, Mungo (her dog) and Midge (a flute-playing mouse).
The Herbs	1970	Parsley the Lion, Dill the Dog, Sage the Owl, Sir Basil and Lady Rosemary, Constable Knapweed, Bayleaf the Gardener etc.

French and German leaders since 1945

Presidents of France	*Period in office*	Chancellor of Germany	*Period in office*
Vincent Auriol	1947-54	Konrad Adenauer	1949-63
René Coty	1954-59	Ludwig Erhard	1963-66
Charles de Gaulle	1959-69	Kurt Georg Kiesinger	1966-69
Georges Pompidou	1969-74	Willy Brandt	1969-74
Valéry Giscard d'Estaing	1974-81	Helmut Schmidt	1974-82
François Mitterrand	1981-95	Helmut Kohl	1982-98
Jacques Chirac	1995-2007	Gerhard Schröder	1998-2005
Nicolas Sarkozy	2007-	Angela Merkel	2005-

Old ways of remembering things

The number of days in the months:
Thirty days hath September, April, June and November. All the rest have thirty-one, except for February alone, which has twenty-eight days clear, and twenty-nine each leap year.

Kings and Queens of England:
Willie, Willie, Harry, Steve,
Harry, Dick, John, Harry three.
One, two, three Neds, Richard two,
Harrys four, five, six... then who?
Edwards four, five, Dick the bad,
Harrys twain and Ned the Lad;
Mary, Bessie, James ye ken,
Charlie, Charlie, James again...
William and Mary, Anna Gloria,
Georges I, II, III, IV, William and Victoria;
Edward seven next, and then
George the fifth in 1910;
Ned the eighth soon abdicated
Then George the sixth was coronated;
After which Elizabeth
And that's the end until her death.

The fates of Henry VIII's six wives in order:
Divorced, beheaded, died, divorced, beheaded, survived.
(Catherine of Aragon, Anne Boleyn, Jane Seymour, Anne of Cleves,
Catherine Howard, Catherine Parr).

To remember which way to adjust your clocks:
Spring ahead, Fall back.

The 12 Disciples:
Peter, Andrew, James and John
Philip and Bartholemew
Thomas next and Matthew too
James the less and Judas the greater
Simon the zealot and Judas the traitor.

Kings and Queens

Kings and Queens of England:

House of Normandy
William I (1066-87)
William II (1087-1100)
Henry I (1100-35)
Stephen (1135-54)

House of Plantagenet
Henry II (1154-89)
Richard I (1189-99)
John (1199-1216)
Louis (1216-17 – disputed!)
Henry III (1216-72)
Edward I (1272-1307)
Edward II (1307-27)
Edward III (1327-77)
Richard II (1377-99)

House of Lancaster
Henry IV (1399-1413)
Henry V (1413-22)
Henry VI (1422-61)

House of York
Edward IV (1461-70)

House of Lancaster (restored)
Henry VI (1470-71)

House of York
Edward IV (1471-83)
Edward V (April 9-June 25, 1483)
Richard III (1483-85)

House of Tudor
Henry VII (1485-1509)
Henry VIII (1509-47)
Edward VI (1547-53)
Jane (July 10-19, 1553 – disputed)
Mary I (1553-58)
Elizabeth I (1558-1603)

Kings/Queens of England & Scotland:

House of Stuart
James I, aka James VI of Scotland (1603-25)
Charles I (1625-49)

The Commonwealth
Oliver Cromwell (1653-58)
Richard Cromwell (1658-59)

House of Stuart (restored)
Charles II (1660-85)
James II, aka James VII of Scotland (1685-88)

House of Orange and Stuart
William III (1689-1702) & Mary II (1689-94).

House of Stuart
Anne (1702-07)

Kings and Queens of Great Britain:

House of Stuart
Anne (1707-14)

House of Hanover
George I (1714-27)
George II (1727-60)
George III (1760-1820)
George IV (1820-30)
William IV (1830-37)
Victoria (1837-1901)

House of Saxe-Coburg-Gotha
Edward VII (1901-10)

House of Windsor
George V (1910-36)
Edward VIII (January 20-December 11, 1936)
George VI (1936-52)
Elizabeth II (1952-)

Kings and Queens continued

Kings and Queens of Scotland (to James VI)

House of Alpin
Kenneth Macalpin, aka Kenneth I (843-58)
Donald I (858-62)
Constantine I (862-78)
Aedh (878-79)
Eochaid (879-89)
Donald II (889-900)
Constantine II (900-42)
Malcolm I (942-54)
Indulph (954-62)
Duff (962-66)
Colin (966-71)
Kenneth II (971-95)
Constantine III (995-97)
Kenneth III (997-1005)
Malcolm II (1005-34)

House of Dunkeld
Duncan I (1034-40)
Macbeth (1040-57)
Lulach (1057-58)
Malcolm III (1058-93)
Donald III (1093-94)
Duncan II (May to November 1094)
Donald III (1094-97)
Edgar (1097-1107)
Alexander I (1107-24)
David I (1124-53)
Malcolm IV (1153-65)
William the Lion (1165-1214)
Alexander II (1214-49)
Alexander III (1249-86)

House of Fairhair
Margaret, the Maid of Norway (1286-90)

House of Balliol
John de Balliol, aka Toom Tabard (1292-96)

House of Bruce
Robert the Bruce, aka Robert I (1306-29)
David II (1329-71)

House of Stuart
Robert II (1371-90)
Robert III (1390-1406)
James I (1406-37)
James II (1437-60)
James III (1460-88)
James IV (1488-1513)
James V (1513-42)
Mary, Queen of Scots (1542-67)
James VI, aka James I of England (1569-1625)

Records "banned" by the BBC

Year	Artist	Song	Reason for ban
1937	George Formby	"My Little Stick Of Blackpool Rock"	Suggestive references to his "little stick of Blackpool rock".
1941	Billie Holiday	"Gloomy Sunday"	Promotion of suicide.
1953	Frankie Laine	"Answer Me"	Mockery of religious prayer.
1956	Lonnie Donegan	"Digging My Potatoes"	Sexual innuendo, for example in the line "Thought you were my friend till I caught you in my bed".
1959	Johnny Horton	"Battle Of New Orleans"	Reference to "The bloody British".
1960	Ricky Valance	"Tell Laura I Love Her"	Morbid reference to dying in a stock car race.
1961	Mike Berry and the Outlaws	"Tribute To Buddy Holly"	Morbid fascination with a dead teen idol.
1966	The Troggs	"I Can't Control Myself"	"Lewdly suggestive sounds" made by singer Reg Presley.
1967	The Beatles	"A Day In The Life"	Drug references.
1967	The Beatles	"Lucy In The Sky With Diamonds"	A schoolboy called Clive Whichelow wrote to Record Mirror on July 1, 1967, noting that the title spelt LSD – the rest is history!
1967	The Rolling Stones	"Let's Spend The Night Together"	Promotion of promiscuity.
1967	Scott Walker	"Jackie"	Risqué lyrics concerning bordellos, "authentic queers" and "phony virgins".
1968	The Smoke	"My Friend Jack"	Drug references.
1968	Pink Floyd	"It Would Be So Nice"	Advertizing (mentioned the Evening Standard).
1969	Max Romeo	"Wet Dream"	Sexual innuendo, although Max claimed the song was about his leaky bedroom ceiling!
1969	Serge Gainsbourg and Jane Birkin	"Je T'Aime (Moi Non Plus)"	Overtly erotic noises – the BBC played an instrumental version instead.
1970	Kinks	"Lola"	Advertizing (original lyrics mentioned "Coca Cola" but were later changed to "Cherry Cola")

FA Cup finalists 1945-80

1945-46	Derby County	4–1	Charlton Athletic
1946-47	Charlton Athletic	1–0	Burnley
1947-48	Manchester United	4–2	Blackpool
1948-49	Wolverhampton Wanderers	3–1	Leicester City
1949-50	Arsenal	2–0	Liverpool
1950-51	Newcastle United	2–0	Blackpool
1951-52	Newcastle United	1–0	Arsenal
1952-53	Blackpool	4–3	Bolton Wanderers
1953-54	West Bromwich Albion	3–2	Preston North End
1954-55	Newcastle United	3–1	Manchester City
1955-56	Manchester City	3–1	Birmingham City
1956-57	Aston Villa	2–1	Manchester United
1957-58	Bolton Wanderers	2–0	Manchester United
1958-59	Nottingham Forest	2–1	Luton Town
1959-60	Wolverhampton Wanderers	3–0	Blackburn Rovers
1960-61	Tottenham Hotspur	2–0	Leicester City
1961-62	Tottenham Hotspur	3–1	Burnley
1962-63	Manchester United	3–1	Leicester City
1963-64	West Ham United	3–2	Preston North End
1964-65	Liverpool	2–1	Leeds United
1965-66	Everton	3–2	Sheffield Wednesday
1966-67	Tottenham Hotspur	2–1	Chelsea
1967-68	West Bromwich Albion	1–0	Everton
1968-69	Manchester City	1–0	Leicester City
1969-70	Chelsea	2–2	Leeds United
1969-70 *(replay)*	Chelsea	2–1	Leeds United
1970-71	Arsenal	2–1	Liverpool
1971-72	Leeds United	1–0	Arsenal
1972-73	Sunderland	1–0	Leeds United
1973-74	Liverpool	3–0	Newcastle United
1974-75	West Ham United	2–0	Fulham
1975-76	Southampton	1–0	Manchester United
1976-77	Manchester United	2–1	Liverpool
1977-78	Ipswich Town	1–0	Arsenal
1978-79	Arsenal	3–2	Manchester United
1979-80	West Ham United	1–0	Arsenal

Home chemistry experiments

Making a stink bomb

- Remove heads from book of matches.
- Place in an empty bottle.
- Add 2 tbsps of household ammonia and seal bottle.
- Leave for 3-4 days.
- Ammonium sulphide will form in the bottle and its rotten egg smell will be ready to be released whenever you remove the bottle top.

Copper sulphate crystals

- Stir copper sulphate into very hot water until no more will dissolve.
- Pour small amount of solution into a shallow dish and leave for a few hours.
- Select best crystal that forms.
- Tie crystal to length of thread and suspend in a clean jar filled with solution made earlier.
- Leave jar undisturbed for several days with paper towel over top.
- Keep checking crystal.
- When you are happy with it, remove it and leave it to dry.

Baking soda and vinegar volcano

- Mix 6 cups flour, 2 cups salt, 4 tbsps cooking oil and 2 cups of water until the mixture is smooth and firm.
- Place plastic drink bottle in baking pan and mould dough around sides.
- Fill bottle ¾ full with warm water.
- Add some food colouring.
- Add 6 drops of detergent to the bottle contents.
- Add 2 tbsps baking soda to the liquid and then slowly pour vinegar into the bottle.
- Stand back while your volcano erupts!

Abbreviations used by doctors

Ash Cash	Money paid for signing a cremation form.
CLL	Complete Low-Life.
CNS – QNS	Central Nervous System – Quantity Not Sufficient.
CTD	Circling the Drain (a patient expected to die soon).
DBI	Dirt Bag Index (number of tattoos x number of missing teeth = number of days since patient last bathed).
Departure Lounge	Geriatric ward.
Digging for Worms	Varicose vein surgery.
FLK	Funny Looking Kid.
FOS	Full Of S***.
GLL	Great-Looking Legs.
GLM	Good-Looking Mum.
GOK	God Only Knows.
GPO	Good for Parts Only.
GROLIES	Guardian Reader Of Low Intelligence In Ethnic Skirt.
Handbag positive	Confused elderly woman lying on the bed but still clutching her handbag.
House red	Blood.
JLD	Just Like Dad.
LOBNH	Lights On But Nobody Home.
LOL	Little Old Lady.
NFN	Normal For Norfolk.
OAP	Over-Anxious Parent.
PDE	P****d, Denies Everything.
PFO	P****d, Fell Over.
PGT	P****d, Got Thumped.
PIB	Pain In the Bum.
PIN	Pain In the Neck.
PRATFO	Patient Reassured And Told to F*** Off.
Pumpkin Positive	If you shine a light in the patient's ear, their whole head will light up.
SIG	Stupid Ignorant Git.
TATT	Tired All The Time.
TBP	Total Bloody Pain.
TEETH	Tried Everything Else, Try Homeopathy.
TTFO	Told To F*** Off.
UBI	Unexplained Beer Injury.
WAW	What A Wally.
Woolworth's test	If you can imagine the patient shopping in Woolies it is safe to give an anaesthetic.
WOT	Waste of Time.

British political leaders who didn't become Prime Minister (so far...)

	Born/died	Period as party leader
Conservative		
William Hague	1961-	1997-2001
Iain Duncan Smith	1954-	2001-03
Michael Howard	1941-	2003-05
Labour		
Hugh Gaitskell	1906-63	1955-63
Michael Foot	1913-2010	1980-83
Neil Kinnock	1942-	1983-92
John Smith	1938-94	1992-94
Ed Miliband	1969	2010
Liberal		
Clement Davies	1884-1962	1945-56
Jo Grimond	1913-93	1956-67
Jeremy Thorpe	1929-	1967-76
David Steel	1938-	1976-88
Social Democratic Party		
Roy Jenkins	1920-2003	1981-83
David Owen	1938-	1983-87
Robert Maclennan	1936-	1987-88
Liberal Democrats		
David Steel (joint leader)	1938-	1988
Robert Maclennan (joint leader)	1936-	1988
Paddy Ashdown	1941-	1988-99
Charles Kennedy	1959-	1999-2006
Menzies Campbell	1941-	2006-07
Nick Clegg	1967-	2007

Lighting the fire in the hearth
pre-central heating

- Clean out the grate, which probably still contained the remains of the last fire – grey ash, strange lumps of coal or some other substance which had mysteriously failed to burn.

- Find some old newspaper and roll it into balls, keeping some back for important use later. Place newspaper balls in grate.

- Go out to the backyard and find the chopper.
  Cut up some kindling wood.

- Put chopped-up wood on top of newspaper – thin bits first, covered by slightly thicker bits.

- Go back out to yard where the coal bunker is situated, remembering to take coal scuttle and little shovel with you. Fill scuttle with coal and take back to fire.

- Carefully balance small pieces of coal on top of wood.

- Find matches and light paper at bottom of pile in several places (try again when flames frustratingly go out).

- Once paper is burning nicely, find the piece of newspaper you have saved and gently fan the flames.

- When the smaller pieces of coal have begun to burn, add larger pieces.

- NB: It was possible to use firelighters, but these weren't cheap and might have been considered by many to be cheating.

- Many houses possessed a little stand next to the fireplace from which hung a little shovel, a matching pair of tongs and a brush. Quite often, at least one of these items would never be used.

Waddingtons' Board Games

Game	First issued	
Lexicon	1933	Card game about words.
Sorry!	1934	Board game based on the ancient cross and circle game pachisi.
Monopoly	1935	The classic property game originally issued by Parker Brothers in the USA.
Totopoly	1938	Horse-racing game using a board, dice and cards.
Buccaneer	1938	A game of piracy on the high seas in which players try to return to their home port with diamonds, rubies, pearls, gold bars and rum barrels.
Cluedo	1949	The classic game of murder, mystery and detection.
Scoop!	1953	A newspaper-based game about collecting stories and making up the front page.
Astron	1954	Players have to land six metal space ships on numbered space stations.
Careers	1957	Players pursue a success formula of fame, happiness or money or a combination of all three.
Risk!	1959	Strategic war game of world domination.
Battle Of The Little Big Horn	1964	Board game featuring Indian chiefs and General Custer and his men.
Kimbo	1961	"The game of fences".
Railroader	1963	Players have to build their railway across the Wild West.
Bonanza Rummy Game	1964	Bonanza TV series themed version of the card game rummy.
Formula 1	1964	Strategy board game based on motor racing.
Spy Ring	1965	Players take the part of spies in the diplomatic quarter of Bludt, in Espiona.
Table Football	1965	Cardboard pitch with two teams of plastic men.
Boobytrap	1967	Take out the discs that are caught in the booby trap without causing the spring bar to snap.
Rat Race	1967	A madcap game of social climbing.
Blast Off	1969	A game of modern space exploration and technology.
Air Charter	1970	Convey freight by aeroplane to small airports in Australasia and South East Asia and make the highest profit.
Cube Fusion	1970	3D noughts and crosses game.
Campaign	1971	Strategy game in which players can become a Napoleon or a Wellington as they lead their armies across Europe.
4000 A.D.	1971	Game of strategy set 2,000 years in the future.
Speculate	1972	Board game of stocks and shares, a game of strategy and investment.
Ulcers	1973	The fun game that gives you power over people.
Project KGB	1973	A frantic game of rival agents on a search assignment.

Literary terms

Alliteration: The repetition of initial consonant sounds,
eg. "Round the rugged rock…"

Antiphrasis: Irony established in one word by means of context,
eg. "Now look what you've done, brainbox!"

Hyperbole: Deliberate exaggeration,
eg. "If I've told you once I've told you a thousand times…"

Litotes: Understatement generated by denying the opposite of what
might normally be said, eg. "It's not so warm outside today."

Meiosis: A euphemistic figure of speech,
eg. speaking of the Northern Ireland "troubles".

Metaphor: A comparison between two different things
achieved by asserting that one thing is another thing,
eg. "I am the bread of life".

Metonymy: a form of metaphor similar to synecdoche in which
something is referred to by the name of something
very closely associated with it, eg. using the word
"Westminster" to refer to the British Parliament.

Onomatopoeia: Words whose pronunciation imitates the sound they describe,
eg. "buzz".

Oxymoron: A paradox in two words,
eg. "That was an expensive bargain".

Simile: A comparison between two different things usually introduced
by the word "like", eg. "My love is like a red, red rose."

Synecdoche : Type of metaphor in which the part stands for the whole
(eg. "threads" used to mean "clothes") or a function stands
for a device (eg "a ride" used to refer to "a vehicle").

Understatement: Deliberately expressing an idea as being less important
than it actually is.

Zeugma: Two or more parts of a sentence are yoked together by a single
common verb or noun, eg. "He left in a huff and a taxicab."

Previous holders of royal titles

Title	Current Holder	Previous holder
The Duke of Edinburgh	**Prince Philip** (from 1947)	Prince Albert (son of Queen Victoria who held the title of Duke of Edinburgh from 1866 to 1893).
The Prince of Wales	**Prince Charles** (from 1958)	Prince Edward (son of George V and uncle to the present Queen who held the title from 1910 until 1936, when he was crowned as King Edward VIII).
Princess Royal	**Princess Anne** (from 1987)	Princess Mary (only daughter of George V and Queen Mary and thus an aunt of the present Queen; held the title from 1932 until her death in 1965).
The Duke of York	**Prince Andrew** (from 1986)	Prince Albert (the present Queen's father, who held the title from 1920 until his accession to the throne as George VI in 1936).
The Earl of Wessex	**Prince Edward** (from 1999)	William FitzOsbern (given the title by William the Conqueror following the death of its previous holder, Harold Godwinson).
The Duke of Cambridge	**Prince William** (from 2011)	Previously Prince George (a grandson of George III and thus cousin of Queen Victoria, who held the title from 1850 until his death in 1904).

Things you may have been called as a youngster

Daft ha'porth • Young whippersnapper • Little tyke
Cheeky monkey • Silly article • Knee-high to a grasshopper
Little perisher • Little blighter • Cheeky beggar • Little so and so

Now less-frequent visitors to the house

- **Coalman** *(bringing deliveries of solid fuel to your coal shed)*.
- **The Corona man** *(bringing supplies of fizzy drinks to your door)*.
- **The door-to-door encyclopedia salesmen** *(trying to sell you large sets of expensive reference tomes)*.
- **The insurance man** *(who would collect your weekly insurance instalment, in cash, before ticking off your little book to show you'd paid)*.
- **The rag-and-bone man** *(now replaced by charity bags stuffed through the letterbox)*.
- **The knife-grinder** *(come to sharpen your knives, scissors and other kitchen and garden equipment)*.

Essential rag-and-bone man equipment

Horse • cart • trumpet or handbell to attract attention
goldfish, balloons, paper windmills, • tin whistles (to give to children in
exchange for suitably sized bundles of old clothes or rags)

The kerb drill

Stand in a place where you can clearly see both ways.
Look right.
Look left.
Look right again.
And, if it's all clear, walk straight across and keep looking.

*As, for example, taught by the Tufty Club, which was founded in
1961 for children under five years old. Tufty Fluffytail himself had been
created in 1953 as a wise red squirrel who imparted safety advice to children.
Enrolment in the Tufty Club cost 2s. 6d. after which members were sent
a club badge featuring Tufty (in blue jacket and yellow trousers), along with
an illustrated book of stories about road safety featuring Tufty and his friends.*

Saturday morning cinema serials

Main character	Sidekicks, enemies, etc	Best known for
Zorro	*Servant:* Bernardo *Enemy:* Sgt Pedro Gonzales	Writing "Z" on walls with his sword.
The Lone Ranger	*Sidekick:* Tonto	"Hi Yo Silver!" and "Who was that masked man?"
The Cisco Kid	*Sidekick:* Pancho	Ending film with a joke and laughing "Oh, Pancho!", "Oh, Cisco!"
Flash Gordon	*Sidekicks:* Dale Arden and Dr Hans Zarkov	Adventures on planet Mongo, battling Ming the Merciless.
Roy Rogers	His horse, Trigger	White hat and snazzy shirt.
Superman	*Girlfriend* Lois Lane and *enemy* Lex Luthor	Being faster than a speeding bullet, more powerful than a locomotive, able to leap tall buildings in a single bound.
Hopalong Cassidy	*Sidekicks:* Windy Halliday, Speedy McGinnis and Clyde	Wearing black (even though he was a goody!)

Note: *If you went to Saturday morning pictures at the ABC you were an*
"ABC Minor" and if you went to the Granada you were a "Grenadier".

Bands from the Trad Jazz boom years

Kenny Ball's Jazzmen • Chris Barber Band
Mr Acker Bilk and His Paramount Jazz Band
Ken Colyer's Jazzmen • Mike Cotton Band •
Humphrey Lyttleton Band • Mick Mulligan's Magnolia Jazz Band
• Monty Sunshine • Alex Welsh Band Storyville Jazzmen
(with Bob Wallis) • Terry Lightfoot and His Jazzmen

TV and radio tie-in toys of the 1950s

Board games

- Beat The Clock (from Spears Games, as seen on *Sunday Night At The London Palladium*).
- *Whacko!* board game (by Chad Valley, based on the TV show with Jimmy Edwards and sold by arrangement with its writers Frank Muir and Denis Norden – "Be dim with Jim in this hilarious game for half-wits").
- The Lone Ranger Chase (from Peter Pan Games).
- *The $64,000 Question* (by Chad Valley).
- *Double Your Money* (from Bells Games – based on "the sensational Hughie Green ITV show").
- *Hancock's Half Hour* board game (by Chad Valley).
- *Take Your Pick* ("based on the exciting ITV quiz game" with Michael Miles).
- *Robin Hood* ("from the exciting ITV show starring Richard Greene").

Other tie-in toys:

- Official *Emergency Ward 10* Nurse's Uniform, as shewn on television (sic).
- Peter Brough's Archie Andrews Ventriloquist Doll by Palitoy (from radio's *Educating Archie*).
- Muffin the Mule push-along toy by Kohnstam.
- Sooty hand puppet by Chad Valley.
- Sooty Super Xylophone.
- Sooty toothbrush flute by Combex.

Skiffle bands of the 1950s

Chas McDevitt Skiffle Group *(with Nancy Whiskey)*
Lonnie Donegan Skiffle Group • Johnny Duncan and the Bluegrass Boys
The Vipers • The Quarrymen *(obscure skiffle band formed by teenagers in Liverpool who became well known a few years later!)*

Sweets found in jars in old-fashioned sweet shops

Acid drops – clear, sour and hard-boiled.

Alphabet letters – shaped like letters of the alphabet.

Aniseed balls – small, brown and with aniseed taste.

Army and Navy sweets – liquorice lozenges.

Barley sugar – Orangey-brown, hard, and with a honey flavour.

Bonbons – boiled sweets in favours such as toffee, strawberry, etc.

Bullseyes – black and white balls.

Butterscotch – hard, toffee-coloured and creamy.

Chocolate brazils – Brazil nuts covered in milk chocolate.

Coconut ice – pink and white chunks of sugary coconut.

Cola cubes – hard, pink, sugar-coated and cola-flavoured.

Cough candy – hard, orange twists with aniseed flavour.

Dew drops – small, hard-boiled sweets in multiple colours.

Dolly mixtures – small sweets in a variety of pastel shades.

Everton mints – black and white and pillow-shaped.

Floral gums – small, hard gums tasting of flowers!

Flying Saucers – sherbet inside a rice-paper shell.

Jelly babies – soft, chewy and in various colours and fruit flavours.

Jelly beans – soft, torpedo-shaped, various colours and flavours.

Lemonade powder – bright yellow crystals.

Liquorice Allsorts – as we know and love, but without the box!

Midget Gems – small, chewy sweets in various colours.

Milk bottles – chewy, white, vanilla-flavoured and bottle-shaped.

Peanut brittle – hard toffee pieces with peanuts in them.

Pontefract cakes – small, round pieces of liquorice.

Sherbet lemons – yellow and lemon-shaped with sherbet in the middle.

Shrimps – softish pink sweets shaped like the eponymous crustacean.

Sports Mix – chewy sweets shaped like pieces of sports equipment.

Strawberries and cream – hard, pink and white.

Sugar almonds – almonds in hard, pastel-coloured casings.

Vanilla fudge – soft toffee with a vanilla flavour.

Winter mixture – humbugs with flavours such as clove.

Gadgets around the house that we no longer have

Kitchen	Washboard, mangle, twin-tub washing machine, gas lighter, meat safe.
Living room	Radiogram, black and white TV, Dansette record player, 78rpm records, crystal set radio, indoor TV aerial.
Cupboard	Trouser press, cobbler's last for home shoe repairs, Brownie box camera, camera tripod, flashgun for the camera, cine camera, Super 8 film, carpet beater.
Around the house	Round-pin plugs and sockets, two- or three-bar electric fires, fan heaters, a phone with a dial, typewriter.
Bedroom	Teasmade.

Goon Show characters

The Goon Show ran on the BBC Home Service for 10 series from May 28, 1951 until January 28, 1960.

Michael Bentine	Professor Osric Pureheart (until July 15, 1952).
Harry Secombe	Neddie Seagoon (*"What what what what what what what?" "Needle nardle noo!" "Ying tong iddle I po!"*)
Spike Milligan	Eccles (*"Hullo dur"*); Miss Minnie Bannister (*"Hen-er-yyy!"*); Count Moriarty (*"Sapristi!"*); Little Jim (*"He's fallen in the water!"*); Jim Spriggs (*"Hello, Jim. Hello, Ji-im"*).
Peter Sellers	Mr Henry Crun (*"Mnk mnk mnk"*); Grytpype-Thynne (*"You silly twisted boy!"*); Major Dennis Bloodnok (*"Eugh, the flies!" "No more curried eggs for me!"*); Bluebottle (*"You filthy rotten swine!" "You have deaded me!"*); Willium (*"'Ere, mate!"*).

Price increases for basic goods over the past century

The table below shows the prices detailed by the Office for National Statistics' Economic Trends for a range of basic grocery items at different times over the past 100 years, together with the most up-to-date prices currently being charged in supermarkets. Pre-1970 prices are shown in both new and old money.

	Flour (1.5kg/ 3lb 4oz)	Unsliced white loaf (800g/ 1lb 12oz)	Sugar (1kg/ 2lb 3oz)
1914	2.3p (5½d)	1.2p (3d)	3p (7¼d)
1947	3.4p (8¼d)	1.9p (4½d)	3.4p (8¼d)
1960	9.8p (1s 11½d)	4.8p (11½d)	7.4p (1s 5¾d)
1970	10.8p (2s 2d)	8.8p (1s 9d)	8.3p (1s 8d)
1980	39p	37p	36p
1990	55p	65p	62p
2000	60p	70p	55p
2013	£1.18	£1.31	95p

	Milk (1 pint)	Cheese (1kg/ 2lb 3oz)	Eggs (per dozen)
1914	0.7p (1¾d)	8.4p (1s 8¼d)	*
1947	1.9p (4½d)	10.6p (2s 1½d)	8.8p
1960	3.3p (8d)	31p (6s 2½d)	29.5p
1970	4.7p (11½d)	40.8p (8s 2d)	23.2p
1980	17p	£2.09	72p
1990	31p	£3.30	£1.21
2000	34p	£5.05	£1.68
2013	46p	£7.72	£2.81

* *figures not available*

Items needed to form your own skiffle group

Cheap Spanish guitar

Washboard Before washing machines, the washboard was a commonplace household item and could be used as a percussion instrument played with a selection of mum's thimbles.

Tea-chest bass Wooden tea-chest with a broom handle stuck into a hole in the top and a piece of string running from the top of the broom handle to the chest.

Then learn three chords – usually C, F, and G7 – from Bert Weedon's *Play In A Day* book, probably the best-selling guitar tutor book ever.

Essential trigonometry

- The sum of the three angles of a triangle is always 180°.
- The longest side of a triangle is always opposite to the largest angle.
- A triangle can only have one angle that is 90° (a right angle) or greater (an obtuse angle).
- Pythagoras' theorem states that in a right-angled triangle, the square of the hypotenuse (the longest side of the triangle opposite the right angle) is equal to the sum of the squares of the opposite two sides.
- In an equilateral triangle, the three sides are equal and the three angles are each 60°.
- An isosceles triangle has two equal sides and two equal angles.
- A scalene triangle has no equal sides and no equal angles.

Supermarkets: a brief history

Shop	Date	Place	
Co-op	1844	Toad Lane, Rochdale	The first co-operative store founded by the Rochdale Pioneers with £28 capital. By 1900, 1,439 co-operative societies had been registered.
Sainsbury's	1869	Drury Lane, London	Set up by John James and Mary Ann Sainsbury as a purveyor of butter, milk and eggs.
Lipton's	1870	Stobcross Street, Anderston, Glasgow	Founded by Thomas Lipton.
David Greig	1888	Brixton	A long-surviving grocery chain.
Morrisons	1899	Bradford, West Yorkshire	Founded by William Morrison as an egg and butter merchant at Rawson Market.
Waitrose	1904	Acton, West London	Founded as a grocery shop by Wallace Waite, Arthur Rose and David Taylor. Taylor left after two years.
MacFisheries	1918	400 independent fish shops bought up all over the country	Founded by William Lever, Viscount Leverhulme.
Tesco	1920	Well Street Market, Hackney	Originally a stall selling surplus groceries founded by Jack Cohen. The Tesco name came four years later, formed from the first two letters of Cohen and the initials of his tea supplier T E Stockwell.
Tesco	1929	Burnt Oak, Edgware, Middlesex	Tesco's first store.
Co-op	1942	Romford, Essex	The UK's first self-service store, opened by the London Co-operative Society. By 1950, 90 per cent of all self-service shops were operated by co-operatives.
Co-op	1948	Manor Park, London	The London Co-operative Society opened the UK's first supermarket.
Asda	1949	Leeds, West Yorkshire	Founded as Associated Dairies and Farm Stores Ltd.
Sainsbury's	1950	Croydon	Sainsbury's first self-service store.
Gateway	1950	Bristol	Had its origins in grocers J H Mills, founded in 1875.
Premier Supermarket	1951	Streatham, South London	Founded by Patrick Galvani.
Fine Fare	1951	Welwyn Garden City, Hertfordshire	Founded as an offshoot of Welwyn Department Stores.
Waitrose	1955	Streatham, South London	The UK's first Waitrose supermarket.
Tesco	1956	St Albans, Hertfordshire	Tesco's first self-service store.
Tesco	1956	Maldon, Essex	Tesco's first supermarket.
Fine Fare	1956	Brighton	Fine Fare's first supermarket.
Morrisons	1958	City centre, Bradford	Morrisons' first self-service store (with three tills!)
Kwik Save	1959	Queen Street, Rhyl	Founded by Albert Gubay as Value Foods.
Gateway	1960	Westbury-on-Trym, Bristol	Gateway's first self-service supermarket.
Morrisons	1961	Girlington, Bradford	Morrisons' first self-service supermarket.
Safeway	1962	Bedford	Established as a subsidiary of the US firm Safeway Inc. Initially traded as Safeway Food Stores.
Queens	1963	Castleford, West Yorkshire	Founded by the Asquith brothers. In 1965 they merged with Associated Dairies and Farm Stores Ltd to form the Asda chain of supermarkets.

Old pub games

Bar billiards

Table has nine holes, and skittles near highest-scoring holes (50, 100 and 200 points).

Aim is to pot balls and score as many points as possible before timer runs out.

If the red ball is potted the score is doubled.

After timer runs out all scores are doubled.

Cribbage

Card game usually played with six cards per person.

Score points for getting to 15 or 31 and getting pairs, runs etc.

Scores are kept using matchsticks or pegs on board of 121 holes.

Players take turns in having an extra hand made up of discarded cards known as the "box".

Ringing the Bull

A metal ring on a string is swung towards a "bull's horn" or hook.

The ring has to stay on to count as a successful throw.

Shove Ha'penny

Pre-decimal halfpennies are shoved across a board with the palm of the hand.

The aim is to get a coin within each of the nine sections of the board three times each.

Every time a coin lands between the lines of a section, a chalk mark is made at the side of the board.

Post-war US and Soviet/Russian leaders

Presidents of the USA

	Period in office
Franklin D Roosevelt (1882-1945)	March 4, 1933-April 12, 1945
Harry S Truman (1884-1972)	April 12, 1945-January 20, 1953
Dwight D Eisenhower (1890-1969)	January 20, 1953-January 20, 1961
John F Kennedy (1917-63)	January 20, 1961-November 22, 1963
Lyndon B Johnson (1908-73)	November 22, 1963-January 20, 1969
Richard Nixon (1913-94)	January 20, 1969-August 9, 1974
Gerald Ford (1913-2006)	August 9, 1974-January 20, 1977
Jimmy Carter (b. 1924)	January 20, 1977-January 20, 1981
Ronald Reagan (1911-2004)	January 20, 1981-January 20, 1989
George H W Bush (b. 1924)	January 20, 1989-January 20, 1993
Bill Clinton (b. 1946)	January 20, 1993-Janaury 20, 2001
George W Bush (b. 1946)	January 20, 2001-January 20, 2009
Barack Obama (b. 1961)	January 20, 2009-

Secretaries of Communist Party of the USSR *Period in office*

Joseph Stalin (1878-1953)	April 3, 1922-October 16, 1952
Nikita Khrushchev (1894-1971)	September 14, 1953-October 14, 1964
Leonid Brezhnev (1906-82)	October 14, 1964-November 10, 1982
Yuri Andropov (1914-84)	November 12, 1982-February 9, 1984
Konstantin Chernenko (1911-85)	February 13, 1984-March 10, 1985
Mikhail Gorbachev (b. 1931)	March 11, 1985-August 24, 1991

President of Russia

Boris Yeltsin (1931-2007)	July 10, 1991-December 31, 1999
Vladimir Putin (b. 1952)	May 7, 2000-May 7, 2008
Dmitry Medvedev (b 1965)	May 7, 2008-May 7, 2012
Vladimir Putin (b. 1952)	May 7, 2012-

Britain's pre-decimal coins

The farthing One quarter of an old penny. The word farthing comes from the Anglo-Saxon word feorthing, which means a fourth part. The coin was first minted in the 13th century and ceased to be legal tender on December 31, 1960. It was about the same size as the current 1p. From 1936 the reverse of the coin showed the image of a wren.

The halfpenny Or ha'penny. About the same size as the current 2p. It dates back as far as the reign of Henry I in the early 12th century. From 1936 the reverse of the coin showed an image of a sailing ship, believed to be based on the *Golden Hind* in which Francis Drake circumnavigated the world. It ceased to be legal tender in 1969.

Britain's pre-decimal coins continued

The penny

First introduced c.785 in the reign of King Offa of Mercia. It was referred to as 1d in reference to the Ancient Roman coin the denarius. The penny was approximately 31mm in diameter and carried an image of Britannia on its reverse. There were 240 pennies to £1 and 12 pennies to a shilling. The final issue of the old penny coins was in 1970 prior to decimalization in 1971.

The threepence

Or thruppence, or thruppenny bit. First appeared in the reign of Edward VI (1547-53). In the years before decimalization, the thruppenny bit was a 12-sided brass coin with an image of a Tudor portcullis with chains and coronet on its reverse. It ceased to be legal tender on August 31, 1971.

The sixpence

Or tanner. First minted in England in 1551, it was worth half of one shilling, 19mm in diameter and remained legal tender until June 30, 1980. Until 1946 the coin was made from 50 per cent silver.

The shilling

There were 20 shillings to a to a pound. The shilling or bob was earlier known as the testoon and was introduced in England during the reign of Henry VII (1485-1509). The last shillings before decimalization carried an image on the reverse of the three lions passant from the English coat of arms. Upon decimalization the shilling was replaced by the 5p coin, which initially was of the same size and weight. The shilling remained in use until 1990, when the 5p was reduced in size.

Two shillings

Or florin. Depicted a Tudor rose surrounded by thistles, shamrocks and leeks. It was replaced following decimalization by the 10p coin, which initially was the same size and weight. The two-shilling coin was withdrawn in 1993 when the 10p was reduced in size.

Half-crown

Was worth 2.5 shillings and was 32mm in diameter. It was first issued in 1549 and was demonetized on January 1, 1970.

Crown

Was worth 5 shillings. It was introduced by Henry VIII in 1526 and was last minted in 1965.

The half-sovereign

Was a 22-carat gold coin, 19.3mm in diameter and worth 10 shillings. It was introduced in 1544 and last produced in 1926. The reverse of the coin showed an image of Saint George slaying the dragon.

Years in which TV music series began

1957	*Six-Five Special*
1958	*Oh Boy!*
1959	*Juke Box Jury*
1961	*Thank Your Lucky Stars*
1963	*Ready Steady Go!*
1964	*Top of the Pops*
1968	*Colour Me Pop*
1969	*Lift Off With Ayesha*
1971	*The Old Grey Whistle Test*

Monaco Grand Prix winners

Year	Driver	Company
1950	Juan Manuel Fangio	Alfa Romeo
1952	Vittorio Marzotto	Ferrari
1955	Maurice Trintignant	Ferrari
1956	Stirling Moss	Maserati
1957	Juan Manuel Fangio	Maserati
1958	Maurice Trintignant	Cooper Climax
1959	Jack Brabham	Cooper Climax
1960	Stirling Moss	Lotus-Climax
1961	Stirling Moss	Lotus-Climax
1962	Bruce McLaren	Cooper Climax
1963	Graham Hill	BRM
1964	Graham Hill	BRM
1965	Graham Hill	BRM
1966	Jackie Stewart	BRM
1967	Denny Hulme	Brabham-Repco
1968	Graham Hill	Lotus-Ford
1969	Graham Hill	Lotus-Ford
1970	Jochen Rindt	Lotus-Ford
1971	Jackie Stewart	Tyrell-Ford
1972	Jean-Pierre Beltoise	BRM
1973	Jackie Stewart	Tyrell-Ford
1974	Ronnie Peterson	Lotus-Ford
1975	Nikki Lauda	Ferrari

Note: Not held in 1951, 1953, 1954

Some 1950s and '60s London coffee bars

The Two I's • Freight Train • Le Grande • Melbray • Sam Widges *(gettit?)*
Picasso • Le Macabre • Las Vegas • Stockpot • Al Tora • Heaven and Hell
Universal • The Goings On • The Moka Bar •

Ingredients for some tasty rationing-era meals

Stewed tripe and onions

1lb tripe
1oz butter
2 large onions
1oz cornflour
½ pint water
salt and pepper
½ pint milk

Spam fritters

For the batter:
4oz plain flour
4 fluid oz milk
1 egg
Pinch of salt
1tbsp of oil

For the Spam:
1 tin of Spam

Semolina pudding

1oz caster sugar
1 egg
1 pint milk
Strip of lemon rind
   or a little cinnamon
1oz semolina

Sugarless cake

4oz margarine
½lb self-raising flour
4oz sweetened
   condensed milk
A little milk
Pinch salt
4oz sultanas
2 dried eggs
   (reconstituted)
¼ tsp ground
   cinammon

Carrot fudge

Carrots
Gelatine
Orange essence

Reconstituted egg on toast

Dried egg
Water
2 slices of bread

The Country Code

Guard against the risk of fire. Great damage is done every year to crops, plantations, woodlands and heaths. A match or cigarette thrown away or a pipe carelessly knocked out, picnic fires not properly extinguished, or lighted near dry crops can quickly start a blaze.

Fasten ALL gates. If animals get out of a field they stray. As a result they may do serious damage to crops, suffer injury on the roads or eat food that is harmful.

Keep dogs under control. Animals are easily frightened, even by small, playful dogs. Stillbirths may be the result.

Keep to the paths across farm land. Crops are damaged by treading; flattened crops are difficult to harvest. Grass is a valuable crop.

Avoid damaging fencing, hedges and walls. If these are damaged, gaps will be caused. Where a person goes, an animal may follow.

Leave NO litter. Litter is not just unsightly, but often a danger as well. Broken glass and tins may injure animals and harm machinery.

Safeguard water supplies. Countrymen often depend on wells and streams for water for themselves and their animals.

Protect wildlife, plants and trees. Wild animals should not be disturbed, plants uprooted nor trees treated roughly.

Go carefully on country roads. If there is no footpath, walkers are generally safer on the right, facing oncoming traffic. Care and patience are needed by motorists when passing farm animals or horses being ridden or otherwise.

Respect the life of the countryside. Many of the machines and much of the business stock on which the farmer depends for his livelihood have to be kept in the open. Take care not to damage them.

Sterling dollar exchange rate through the past century

1900	1910	1920	1930	1940	1950
$4.87	$4.86	$3.66	$4.86	$3.83	$2.80

1960	1970	1980	1990	2000	2013
$2.81	$2.40	$2.33	$1.78	$1.52	$1.52

Old school dreads

The nit nurse "Nitty Nora, the bug explorer" would visit the school two or three times a year and inspect the heads of the children with the aid of a fine-toothed comb. If head lice were discovered, parents would be informed and advised to treat with a special lotion.

Vaccinations Tales of children being scarred for life by the BCG (Bacille Calmette-Guérin) injection terrified everyone. In reality, it meant a small inoculation mark afterwards.

Truancy officer If you bunked or sagged off school, this was the man (sometimes in uniform) who would round you up again.

11-plus Brought in by the Education Act of 1944, the 11-plus loomed large in the future for all children approaching the end of junior school. It consisted of three parts: writing, arithmetic and general problem-solving. The results determined whether you would go to a grammar school or a secondary modern school, and in those more class-conscious days significantly affected future life chances for many.

Lines If your misdemeanour was not quite bad enough to warrant detention or the cane, then it was lines – writing out "I must not...." 50, 100, or perhaps even 500 times.

Starting dates of TV drama series

1953   *The Quatermass Experiment*

1955   *Dixon Of Dock Green;*
The Adventures
   of Robin Hood

1956   *Armchair Theatre;*
Gunsmoke

1957   *Emergency Ward 10*

1959   *Laramie;*
Rawhide

1960   *Bonanza;*
Coronation Street;
Danger Man; Maigret

1961   *The Avengers;*
Ben Casey;
Perry Mason

1962   *Doctor Finlay's Casebook;*
The Saint;
Z Cars

1963   *Doctor Who;*
The Twilight Zone

1964   *Crossroads;*
The Outer Limits;
The Virginian;
The Wednesday Play

1965   *Lost in Space;*
The Man From Uncle

1966   *Adam Adamant Lives!;*
The Baron;
Batman;
Softly, Softly

1967   *Callan;*
The Forsyte Saga;
A Man Called Ironside;
The Prisoner;
Tarzan

1968   *The Champions;*
Land of the Giants;
The Time Tunnel

1969   *Department S;*
Paul Temple;
Randall and Hopkirk
   (Deceased);
Star Trek

1970   *A Family At War;*
Hawaii Five-0;
Mission Impossible;
The Six Wives of Henry VIII

1971   *Elizabeth R; Jason King;*
The Onedin Line;
The Persuaders;
Upstairs, Downstairs

1972   *Cannon; Colditz;*
Crown Court;
Emmerdale Farm

1973   *The Streets of San Francisco*

1974   *Kojak;*
The Six Million Dollar Man

1975   *Little House on the Prairie;*
Rumpole of the Bailey;
Poldark; Survivors

1976   *Bouquet of Barbed Wire;*
The Duchess of Duke Street;
I, Claudius;
The New Avengers;
Starsky and Hutch;
When the Boat Comes In

1977   *The Professionals*

1978   *All Creatures Great and Small;*
Dallas;
Pennies From Heaven

For US-made series, starting dates shown are for first broadcast in UK.

British land speed records

February 4, 1927: Malcolm Campbell drove *Bluebird* at 174.883 mph on the beach at Pendine Sands, South Wales.

March 11, 1929: Major Henry Seagrave set a land speed record of 231.446 mph at Daytona Beach, Florida, in the 1,000hp Sunbeam *Golden Arrow*.

September 3, 1935: Malcolm Campbell averaged 301.129 mph at the Bonneville Salt Flats, Utah, in the Campbell Rolls-Royce *Bluebird*.

November 19, 1937: Captain George Eyston set a record of 312.00 mph at the Bonneville Salt Flats, Utah, in *Thunderbolt*, powered by two Rolls-Royce engines totalling 73 litres.

August 27, 1938: Captain George Eyston set a new record of 345.50 mph.

September 15, 1938: John R Cobb achieved 353.30 mph in the *Railton Special*.

September 16, 1938: Less than 24 hours after Cobb's record, Eyston set a new record of 357.50 mph.

August 23, 1939: Cobb regained the record with a speed of 369.70 mph.

September 16, 1947: Cobb set a new record of 394.196 mph in the *Railton Mobil Special* at Bonneville Salt Flats.

July 17, 1964: Donald Campbell achieved 403.10 mph in the *Bluebird-Proteus* CN7 at Lake Eyre, Australia

Car registration years
(letter at start of registration)

A	B	C	D	E	F	G	H	J	K	L
1983	1984	1985	1986	1987	1988	1989	1990	1991	1992	1993

M	N	P	R	S	T	V	W	X	Y
1994	1995	1996	1997	1998	1999	1999	2000	2000	2001

Toys you could make for yourself

Go-kart

1) Take one plank.
2) Nail one orange box to the top for a seat.
3) Fit old pram wheels to each end of plank.
4) Attach rope to front wheel shaft for steering.
5) Use feet as brakes!

Catapult

1) Find short-forked stick.
2) Cut up old bicycle inner tube for rubber.
3) Cut tongue out of old shoe.
4) Thread rubber through holes made in shoe tongue
    and tie to each side of forked stick.
5) Find target!

Tin-can telephone

1) Ask mum for two old tin cans.
2) Make small hole in bottom of each can.
3) Poke strong thread through and tie a knot on inside of each can.
4) Give one can to friend and walk away from each other until thread is taut.
5) Hold secret conversations regarding your spy network.

Bow and arrow

1) Buy bamboo cane and garden sticks from hardware shop.
2) Attach string to each end of cane so it is taut and bent into a bow.
3) Cut a nick into ends of sticks and use as arrows!

Some more Saturday morning cinema favourites

Abbott and Costello • Bugs Bunny • Jet Morgan • Laurel and Hardy
Mickey Mouse • Rin-Tin-Tin • Tweety Pie and Sylvester

Cinemas you may have visited

ABC • Adelphi • Astoria • Classic • Coliseum • Dominion
Electric • Embassy • Essoldo • Gaumont • Grand • Granada
Majestic • Mayfair • Odeon • Palace • Paramount • Plaza
Regal • Regent • Rex • Rialto • Roxy • Vogue

Now little-used names for parts of the house

Scullery • sitting room • drawing room • lavatory
potting shed • outside toilet • larder • parlour • kitchenette

And some things you may no longer have around the place

Antimacassars and sofa arm covers • coin-in-the-slot electricity and gas meters
doilies • eiderdowns • flying ducks • flypaper • hard toilet paper
hatstand • quilts • stair rods • pelmets

Dates famous toys were invented

The Slinky (*1943*, by American naval engineer Richard James).

Silly Putty (*1943*, by General Electric engineer James Wright,
although not manufactured as a toy until the 1950s).

Lego (*1947*, by Ole Kirk Christiansen).

Mr Potato Head (*1952*, by Hasbro; the original set required
a real potato to fix the parts into).

Play-Doh (*1955*, by Joseph and Noah McVicker, having been originally
developed by Noah as a wallpaper cleaner in the 1930s).

The Space Hopper (*1968*, by Aqualino Cosani).

The UK's first pop chart

- Appeared in the *New Musical Express* on November 14, 1952.

- The first chart was just a top 12.

- Detailed the best-selling singles for the week ending November 8, 1952.

- Although nominally a top 12, the chart comprised 15 records! Two records tied for the number seven, number eight and number 11 positions.

- The chart included Jo Stafford (2), Nat "King" Cole (3), Bing Crosby (4), Guy Mitchell (5), Rosemary Clooney (6), Ray Martin (8), Max Bygraves (11), Mario Lanza (11) and Johnnie Ray (12).

- Frankie Laine had "High Noon" at number seven as well as being at number eight duetting with Doris Day on "Sugar Bush".

- Vera Lynn had three records in the chart: "Forget-Me-Not" (joint number 7), "Homing Waltz" (9) and "Auf Wiedersehn" (10).

- The nation's big number one was Al Martino with "Here In My Heart" on the Capitol label.

Earlier-generation TV cooks

Philip Harben: Started on the wireless in 1942; presented *Cookery* on TV from 1946-51. Trademarks: striped apron and beard.

Fanny Cradock: Real name Phyllis Nan Sortain Pechey. Started as a food columnist for the *Daily Telegraph*. BBC TV series started in 1955. Trademarks: lots of make-up and evening gowns, and her sidekick, monocle-wearing husband Johnnie.

Graham Kerr: TV series *The Galloping Gourmet* started in 1969. Trademarks: drinking wine while cooking and plucking a woman from the audience to sample his food.

Bus travel – old-style

Trolley buses

- First ones were in Bradford and Leeds.
- Trolley poles on top of buses received electricity from overhead wires.
- User will remember them occasionally conking out.
- London trolley buses finished in May 1962.
- The last trolley bus to run was in Bradford.

Conductors

- Conductors wore uniforms with peaked caps.
- Dispensed tickets from a machine slung round their necks.
- Helped passengers on and off with luggage, children, etc.
- Would pull a bellwire to let driver know when to leave bus stop.
- Would shout "Hold very tight now" as bus drew away.

No door

- Old Routemaster buses had no door, just a pole to grab as you jumped on and off – often while the bus was moving.

Smoking upstairs

- Until 1991 it was permissible to smoke upstairs on a double-decker bus.
- There was a "stubber" fixed to the back of seats.

Secretaries-General of the United Nations

	Nationality	Period in office
Trygve Lie	Norwegian	1946-52
Dag Hammarskjöld	Swedish	1953-61
U Thant	Burmese	1961-71
Kurt Waldheim	Austrian	1972-81
Javier Pérez de Cuéllar	Peruvian	1982-91
Boutros Boutros Ghali	Egyptian	1992-97
Kofi Annan	Ghanaian	1997-2006
Ban Ki-moon	South Korean	2007-

Home décor choices we once embraced

Distemper

- Cheap, cheerful and chalky alternative to paint.
- Quite a favourite in the cash-strapped post-war years.

Artex

- "Artex" was the registered trademark of Artex Ltd.
- It has since become a generic term for that material often used to cover ceilings in the 1970s.
- The decorator could create a swirly pattern in white Artex that was reminiscent of a Mr Whippy ice cream.

Stone cladding

- There was a fashion in the 1970s for stone cladding. This involved attaching lumps of stone or fake stone to the outside of your house and covering up perfectly attractive brickwork.

Pebbledash

- Another way of covering up perfectly good brickwork, this involved spraying the exterior walls of your house with bits of gravel stuck into liquid cement.

Door covers

- By the 1960s panelled doors were considered a bit old-fashioned so discerning home-owners would cover the entire door with a lump of hardboard. Très chic!

Famous agony aunts

Evelyn Home (Peggy Makins), b. 1916: *Woman* (1930s to 1950s).
Marjorie Proops (1911-1996): *Daily Mirror* (1960s to 1990s).
Mary Grant (Angela Willans): *Woman's Own* (1960s to 1990s).
Anna Raeburn (born 1944): *Woman* (late 1960s and 19870s).
Claire Rayner (1931-2010): *Woman's Own* (1960s and 1970s).

Inventions from 1950 onward

1950 The credit card.

1951 Super glue;
the video recorder.

1952 The bar code.

1953 The synthesizer;
the black box flight recorder;
the transistor radio.

1954 The non-stick pan;
the oral contraceptive pill;
automatically opening doors;
McDonald's.

1956 The computer hard disk;
the hovercraft;
liquid paper.

1958 The laser.

1959 The pacemaker;
the microchip;
the Barbie doll.

1961 Valium.

1962 The audio cassette;
the fibre-tip pen;
silicone breast implants.

1963 The video disc.

1965 Astroturf;
soft contact lenses;
the compact disc.

1967 The handheld electronic
calculator.

1968 The computer mouse.

1969 The ATM cashpoint machine;
the bar-code scanner;
the ARPAnet academic network
(first step toward the Internet).

1970 The floppy disk.

1971 The food processor;
the LCD (liquid crystal display);
the microprocessor;
the video cassette.

1972 The word processor;
the first video game (Pong).

1973 The disposable lighter.

1974 The Post-it note; liposuction.

1975 The laser printer;
the drink can push-through tab.

1976 The ink-jet printer.

1979 The Walkman;
rollerblades.

1981 The IBM-PC.

1984 The CD-ROM;
the Apple Macintosh.

1985 Microsoft Windows.

1986 The disposable camera.

1988 Prozac.

1989 High-definition television.

1990 The World Wide Web.

1995 The DVD.

1998 Viagra.

2001 The iPod.

Great ocean liners

Queen Mary

- Launched in 1936.
- Named after Mary of Teck, consort of King George V.
- Sailed the route from Southampton to New York via Cherbourg.
- Run by the Cunard line.
- Served as a troopship in World War 2.
- Retired in 1967.
- Now permanently moored in Long Beach, California, and houses a hotel, museum and restaurants.

RMS Queen Elizabeth

- Launched in 1938.
- Named after Queen Elizabeth, consort to King George VI and known latterly as the Queen Mother.
- Sailed the route from Southampton to New York via Cherbourg.
- Run by the Cunard line.
- Carried Royal Mail for 20 years.
- Retired in 1968.
- Sold to Tun Chao Yung for use as a floating university.
- Scrapped after disastrous fire in 1972.

QE2

- Launched in 1969.
- Named after Queen Elizabeth II.
- Sailed the route from Southampton to New York.
- Run by the Cunard line.
- Retired in 2008.
- Bought by Dubai investment company Istithmar.
- Plans to convert to floating hotel.

Ealing comedies

Year	Title	Director	Main Actors
1947	*Hue and Cry*	Charles Crichton	Alastair Sim, Harry Fowler
1948	*Another Shore*	Charles Crichton	Robert Beatty, Moira Lister
1949	*Passport to Pimlico*	Henry Cornelius	Stanley Holloway, Marg. Rutherford
1949	*Whiskey Galore!*	Alexander Mackendrick	Basil Radford, Bruce Seton
1949	*Kind Hearts and Coronets*	Robert Hamer	Dennis Price, Valerie Hobson
1949	*A Run For Your Money*	Charles Frend	Donald Houston, Meredith Edwards
1950	*The Magnet*	Michael Balcon	Stephen Murray, Kay Walsh
1951	*The Lavender Hill Mob*	Charles Crichton	Alec Guinness, Stanley Holloway
1951	*The Man in the White Suit*	Alexander Mackendrick	Alec Guinness, Joan Greenwood
1953	*The Titfield Thunderbolt*	Charles Crichton	Stanley Holloway, George Relph
1953	*Meet Mr Lucifer*	Anthony Pelissier	Stanley Holloway, Peggy Cummins
1954	*The Love Lottery*	Charles Crichton	David Niven, Peggy Cummins
1954	*The Maggie*	Alexander Mackendrick	Alex Mackenzie, Paul Douglas
1955	*The Ladykillers*	Alexander Mackendrick	Alec Guinness, Cecil Parker
1956	*Who Done It?*	Basil Dearden	Benny Hill, Belinda Lee
1957	*Barnacle Bill*	Charles Frend	Alec Guinness, Irene Browne
1957	*Davy*	Michael Relph	Harry Secombe, Alexander Knox

I-Spy Books

The I-Spy paperback books appeared from 1948. They were priced at 6d each and encouraged children to spot everything from birds to churches.

The books were supposedly written by a Red Indian chief called Big Chief I-Spy whose real identity turned out to be that of schoolteacher Charles Warrell. Similarly, the I-Spy head office was either the Wigwam-by-the-Water or the Wigwam-by-the-Green (the latter in fact being on the Edgware Road).

When you had successfully spotted and ticked off everything in your book you could send it to Big Chief I-Spy for a feather and an order of merit certificate.

The original I-Spy titles:

At the Seaside	The Army
On the Farm	The Wheel
History	Sport
On A Train Journey	People and Places
Dogs	Musical Instruments
In the Country	Men At Work
At the Zoo – Animals	Antique Furniture
At the Zoo – Birds and Reptiles	The Universe
In the Street	Road Transport
On the Road	Town Crafts
The Sights Of London	Country Crafts
Horses and Ponies	The Sky
Ships and Harbours	People In Uniform
Boats and Waterways	Motorcycles and Cycles
Aircraft	Bridges
Cars	Sports Cars

Some comics and magazines for girls

Boyfriend   Launched spring 1959. Fashion, pop music and strip
               cartoon love stories with titles such as "I'll Wait For You".

Bunty   First issued 1958. Included a long-running serial called "The
               Four Marys", about a boarding school in Elmbury. In the
               early days it also featured a serial entitled "The Dancing Life
               Of Moira Kent".

Jinty   Published from 1974. Ran a serial entitled "Pam of Pond Hill
               Comprehensive".

Judy   A "picture story paper" launched in January 1960, when
               it included "Sandra of the Secret Ballet School", "The Lass
               of Flinty Farm", "The Runaway Princess", "Nanette of the
               North" and "The Ring That Winks".

Mandy   Began January 1967. Included stories such as "Mary, Maid
               of All Work", "Hockey Hannah" and "The Girls of Knock-
               out Academy".

Romeo   From 1957. Tagline: "For Young Romance". It included
               one-off love stories with titles such as "Maybe This Saturday
               Night", strips such as "Sandie" and the odd pin-up.

And not forgetting: *Tammy* (from 1971), *Girl* (from 1951, sister title to *Eagle*),
Valentine (from 1957), *Mirabelle* (from 1956), *Honey* (from 1960), *Marty*,
Marilyn, *Roxy* (from 1958), *19* (from 1968), *Date* (from 1960), *Jackie* (from
1962), *Petticoat* (from 1966), *My Guy* (from 1978), *Blue Jeans* (from 1977),
Diana (from 1963), *Crystal*, *Princess* (from 1960)...

Petrol prices since 1896

1896   9d per gallon for what we would now call 4-star.
That's 3.75p per gallon in today's money; there are approximately
4.55 litres in a gallon, so that's less than 1p per litre.
Also, there was no tax on petrol at this stage.

1909   1 shilling 1½d per gallon, less than 6p per gallon;
the price now included tax introduced at 3d per gallon
– 21.4% of the total price.

1914   1s 8d per gallon – that's about 8.5p.

1918   3s 7½d per gallon: a leap to about 18p.
Tax is now 13.79%, having been 24% in 1915.

1928   1s 2½d per gallon. In 1920 Liberal PM Lloyd George had
removed the tax on petrol and introduced road tax instead.

1929   1s 7d per gallon. Conservative PM Stanley Baldwin re introduced
road tax at 21%.

1945   2s per gallon; that's 10p per gallon or 2.2p per litre,
and that's with tax at 37.5%.

1956   5s 4d per gallon, about 26.5p; a price peak around the time
of the Suez Crisis. This included 56.25% tax.

1963   4s 9d per gallon; tax is now 57.89%.

1966   5s 5d per gallon; tax is 60%.

1971   34.25p per gallon (following decimalization, we're into new pence;
it would have been about 6s 11d in old money

1974   49.6p per gallon; tax is now down to 51.56%.

1975   73.2p per gallon; the 1970s oil crisis had hit.

1979   98.25p per gallon. Within the following year the price not only crashed
through the £1-a-gallon barrier, but reached 128.5p
– or 28.26p per litre.

1985   199.8p per gallon; tax is now 54%.

1990   213.5p per gallon of 4-star – but now you can get unleaded
for just 194.4p per gallon.

1995   273.4p per gallon, about 60p per litre; tax is 75.41%,
Unleaded is 246.38p per gallon, about 54p per litre.

2000   389p per gallon; 367.19p per gallon for unleaded, tax at 74.84%.

2010   121.9p per litre for unleaded, including 62% tax;
that's about £5.54 per gallon.

2013   133.p per litre for unleaded (at the time of writing;
that's £6.05 per gallon, a 16,023% increase since 1896).

Celebrities who had multiple marriages

Zsa Zsa Gabor	Burhan Asaf Belge (1937-41); Conrad Hilton (1942-47); George Sanders (1949-54); Herbert Hutner (1962-66); Joshua Cosden Jr (1966-67); Jack Ryan (1975-76); Michael O'Hara (1976-83); Felipe de Alba (1983); Frédéric, Prinz von Anhalt (1986-).
Elizabeth Taylor	Conrad Hilton (1950-51); Michael Wilding (1952-57); Michael Todd (1957-58); Eddie Fisher (1959-64); Richard Burton (1964-74); Richard Burton (1975-76); John Warner (1976-82); Larry Fortensky (1991-96).
Artie Shaw	Jane Cairns (1932-33); Mary Allen (1934-37); Lana Turner (1940); Betty Kern (1942-43); Ava Gardner (1945-46); Kathleen Winsor (1946-48); Doris Dowling (1952-56); Evelyn Keyes (1957-85).
Lana Turner	Artie Shaw (1940); Joseph Crane (1942-43); Joseph Crane (1943-44); Henry Topping Jr (1948-52); Lex Barker (1953-57); Fred May (1960-62); Robert P Eaton (1965); Ronald Pellar (1969-72).
Mickey Rooney	Ava Gardner (1942-43); Betty Jane Rase (1944-49); Martha Vickers (1949-51); Elaine Devry (1952-58); Barbara Ann Thomason (1958-66); Marge Lane (1966-67); Carolyn Hockett (1969-75); Jan Chamberlin (1978-).
Joan Collins	Maxwell Reed (1952-56); Anthony Newley (1963-70); Ron Kass (1972-83); Peter Holm (1985-87); Percy Gibson (2002-).
Frank Sinatra	Nancy Barbato (1939-51); Ava Gardner (1951-57); Mia Farrow (1966-68); Barbara Marx (1976-98).
Marilyn Monroe	James Dougherty (1942-46); Joe DiMaggio (1954); Arthur Miller (1956-61).

Chemistry: the table of elements

Atomic no.	Name	Symbol	Yr of discovery	Atomic no	Name	Symbol	Year of discover
1	Hydrogen	H	1776	48	Cadmium	Cd	1817
2	Helium	He	1895	49	Indium	In	1863
3	Lithium	Li	1817	50	Tin	Sn	ancient
4	Beryllium	Be	1797	51	Antimony	Sb	ancient
5	Boron	B	1808	52	Tellurium	Te	1783
6	Carbon	C	ancient	53	Iodine	I	1811
7	Nitrogen	N	1772	54	Xenon	Xe	1898
8	Oxygen	O	1774	55	Caesium	Cs	1860
9	Fluorine	F	1886	56	Barium	Ba	1808
10	Neon	Ne	1898	57	Lanthanum	La	1839
11	Sodium	Na	1807	58	Cerium	Ce	1803
12	Magnesium	Mg	1755	59	Praseodymium	Pr	1885
13	Aluminium	Al	1825	60	Neodymium	Nd	1885
14	Silicon	Si	1824	61	Promethium	Pm	1945
15	Phosphorus	P	1669	62	Samarium	Sm	1879
16	Sulphur	S	ancient	63	Europium	Eu	1901
17	Chlorine	Cl	1774	64	Gadolinium	Gd	1880
18	Argon	Ar	1894	65	Terbium	Tb	1843
19	Potassium	K	1807	66	Dysprosium	Dy	1886
20	Calcium	Ca	1808	67	Holmium	Ho	1867
21	Scandium	Sc	1879	68	Erbium	Er	1842
22	Titanium	Ti	1791	69	Thulium	Tm	1879
23	Vanadium	V	1830	70	Ytterbium	Yb	1878
24	Chromium	Cr	1797	71	Lutetium	Lu	1907
25	Manganese	Mn	1774	72	Hafnium	Hf	1923
26	Iron	Fe	ancient	73	Tantalum	Ta	1802
27	Cobalt	Co	1735	74	Tungsten	W	1783
28	Nickel	Ni	1751	75	Rhenium	Re	1925
29	Copper	Cu	ancient	76	Osmium	Os	1803
30	Zinc	Zn	ancient	77	Iridium	Ir	1803
31	Gallium	Ga	1875	78	Platinum	Pt	1735
32	Germanium	Ge	1886	79	Gold	Au	ancient
33	Arsenic	As	ancient	80	Mercury	Hg	ancient
34	Selenium	Se	1817	81	Thallium	Tl	1861
35	Bromine	Br	1826	82	Lead	Pb	ancient
36	Krypton	Kr	1898	83	Bismuth	Bi	ancient
37	Rubidium	Rb	1861	84	Polonium	Po	1898
38	Strontium	Sr	1790	85	Astatine	At	1940
39	Yttrium	Y	1794	86	Radon	Rn	1900
40	Zirconium	Zr	1789	87	Francium	Fr	1939
41	Niobium	Nb	1801	88	Radium	Ra	1898
42	Molybdenum	Mo	1781	89	Actinium	Ac	1899
43	Technetium	Tc	1937	90	Thorium	Th	1829
44	Ruthenium	Ru	1844	91	Protactinium	Pa	1913
45	Rhodium	Rh	1803	92	Uranium	U	1789
46	Palladium	Pd	1803	93	Neptunium	Np	1940
47	Silver	Ag	ancient	94	Plutonium	Pu	1940

The atomic number of an element = the number of protons in its nucleus.
The nucleus contains protons and neutrons.
If the element is neutral *(ie. has no electrical charge)*
the number of electrons is equal to the number of protons.

Things that were part of driving in the good old days

Running boards

When cars were a little higher off the ground, these could be used to aid stepping into the vehicle.

Physical indicators

Before the advent of flashing light indicators, these little orange pieces of plastic would ping out at the touch of a button.

Starting handles

In the days before engines were quite as reliable as they are now, this was an essential piece of a driver's equipment. Simply poke one end into the hole at front of the car and turn vigorously as if winding up a giant clockwork car.

Push-starting

If you didn't have your starting handle this was Plan B for a non-starting car.

Cigarette lighters and ashtrays

In the days when it seemed that almost everyone smoked, these were as essential as seats or steering wheels.

Double de-clutching

Before the wonders of synchromesh gearboxes drivers had to perform this slightly more complex manoeuvre involving going into neutral first before changing gear, and therefore having to push the clutch down twice.

Essential mathematics: circles

Radius = distance from centre of a circle to its edge.

Diameter = distance of straight line across circle going through centre (diameter = 2 x radius).

Circumference = distance around edge of circle.

Circumference ÷ diameter = π.

π = 22/7 or 3.14159265358979323846264338327950288419716 9...

(the value of π can be calculated to a trillion places without any pattern emerging).

Circumference of circle = π x diameter *or* 2 x π x radius (2πr).

Area of circle = π x the radius squared (πr^2).

Advertising slogans from our youth: soft drinks

- Emigrate to Canada Dry.
- Lovely Jubbly (Jubbly orange drink).
- Things go better with Coca Cola, things go better with Coke.
- It's the real thing (Coca Cola).
- Corona — sparkles up with joy, Corona — for every girl and boy.
- Cresta – it's frothy, man.
- I drink Idris when I's dry.
- We all adore a Kia-Ora.
- Come alive – you're in the Pepsi generation.
- Lipsmackin'thirstquenchin'acetastin'motivatin'goodbuzzin'cooltalkin'highwalkin'fastlivin'evergivin'coolfizzin' – Pepsi!
- I'm a secret lemonade drinker (R. White's lemonade).
- Schhh... you know who (Schweppes).
- Drink Tizer – the appetizer.

Elvis Presley's first single releases

July 19, 1954	"That's All Right"/"Blue Moon of Kentucky" (Sun)
September 25, 1954	"Good Rockin' Tonight"/"I Don't Care If The Sun Don't Shine" (Sun)
December 28, 1954	"Milkcow Blues Boogie"/"You're A Heartbreaker" (Sun)
April 10, 1955	"Baby, Let's Play House"/ "I'm Left, You're Right, She's Gone" (Sun)
August 6, 1955	"I Forgot To Remember To Forget"/ "Mystery Train" (Sun)
January 27, 1956	"Heartbreak Hotel"/ "I Was The One"(RCA)
May 12, 1956	"I Want You, I Need You, I Love You"/ "My Baby Left Me" (RCA)
July 13, 1956	"Don't Be Cruel"/ "Hound Dog" (RCA)
September 8, 1956	"Shake, Rattle and Roll"/ "Lawdy Miss Clawdy" (RCA)
September 8, 1956	"Blue Suede Shoes"/ "Tutti Frutti" (RCA)
September 8, 1956	"I Got A Woman"/ "I'm Counting On You" (RCA)
September 8, 1956	"I'll Never Let You Go" (Little Darlin')/ "I'm Gonna Sit Right Down And Cry (Over You)" (RCA)
September 8, 1956	"Tryin' To Get To You"/ "I Love You Because" (RCA)
September 8, 1956	"Blue Moon"/ "Just Because" (RCA)
September 8, 1956	"Money Honey"/ "One Sided Love Affair" (RCA)
October 6, 1956	"Love Me Tender"/ "Any Way You Want Me" (RCA)
January 4, 1957	"Too Much"/ "Playing For Keeps" (RCA)
March 22, 1957	"All Shook Up"/ "That's When Your Heartaches Begin" (RCA)
June 11, 1957	"Teddy Bear"/ "Loving You" (RCA)
September 24, 1957	"Jailhouse Rock"/ "Treat Me Nice" (RCA)

Note: *RCA took the unusual decision of releasing Elvis' entire first LP in the form of singles – hence the large number of releases on September 8, 1956.*

"Angry Young Men" of the 1950s

Writer	Key Works	
John Osborne	*Look Back in Anger*	(1956)
	The Entertainer	(1957)
John Braine	*Room at the Top*	(1957)
	Life at the Top	(1962)
Alan Sillitoe	*Saturday Night and Sunday Morning*	(1958)
	The Loneliness of the Long-Distance Runner	(1959)
Arnold Wesker	*Chicken Soup With Barley*	(1958)
	Chips With Everything	(1962)
Harold Pinter	*The Birthday Party*	(1957)
	The Caretaker	(1959)
Kingsley Amis	*Lucky Jim*	(1954)
	Take a Girl Like You	(1960)
Colin Wilson	*The Outsider*	(1956)
	Adrift in Soho	(1961)

Early UK visits by American rock 'n' rollers

1957 Bill Haley   1958 Jerry Lee Lewis   1958 Buddy Holly

1959 Gene Vincent   1960 Eddie Cochran   1962 Little Richard

1964 Chuck Berry

NOTE: *In 2008 it was claimed that Elvis had
been shown round London for a day in
1958 by British rocker Tommy Steele.*

TV interlude films of the 1950s

The potter's wheel • A kitten playing with some wool • The spinning wheel
Angelfish • Ploughing • A windmill • Loch reflections • Tapestry work
River and birds • Sea and rocks

Snowiest UK winters since the war

1946-47   Following a mild spell over Christmas and early January, there was continuous snow cover from January 22 to March 17. Every day during this period snow fell somewhere in the UK. The winter was not the coldest of the 20th century but it was certainly one of the snowiest. Much of Devon was left isolated following blizzards, requiring the RAF to drop supplies in some areas.

1950-51   On December 15 there was heavy snow on the south and east coasts with, for example, 15 inches falling in the Isle of Wight in 3.5 hours. At high levels the snow lasted for almost three weeks longer than it had during the winter of 1946-47.

1954-55   Five feet of snow in Lancashire and Yorkshire in January, as well as heavy falls in Scotland. The high Pennines saw snow as late as mid-May.

1957-58   Twenty-three inches of snow fell in Shoeburyness, Essex.

1962-63   Following a terrible fog in London in early December and Glasgow's first white Christmas since 1938, an extremely cold period began on Boxing Day with blizzards in the south of England. Widespread falls of snow occurred in January with two feet of snow in Devon and the north-east and in Braemar, Scotland, the temperature plunged to minus 22.2° centigrade. Farm animals starved because farmers were unable to reach them. The sea froze in places such as Poole in Dorset, the Thames began to freeze and the Cam froze over allowing Cambridge University students to skate 15 miles to Ely.

1965-66   Snow in most areas in November, then more in January in the east, in February in the north-east and heavy falls in the north in April.

1968-69   Heavy snow in east Yorkshire in January with more snow in England and Wales in February and over the Pennines in March.

1969-70   Most parts saw snow during the course of the winter while 12 inches fell on the Midlands.

1977-78   Heavy snow in Scotland in January with falls of up to 28 inches. Snow then fell heavily in the north-east, east and south-west in February.

1978-79   Snow fell in late December in Southern Scotland and the north-east. In February there were drifts of up to seven feet on the east coast and 15 feet in the north-east in March.

Important dates in the history of sliced bread

1928 A bread-slicing machine, invented by Otto Rohwedder,
is exhibited for the first time at a bakery trade fair in the USA.

1930 Sliced bread begins to appear in UK shops as large bakeries
begin using commercial slicers.

1933 The phrase "The best thing since sliced bread" is first used,
while by now around 80% of US bread is pre-sliced and wrapped.

1936 Mother's Pride first appears in Scotland.

1937 Wonderloaf appears – possibly the first nationally available sliced loaf.

1941 In the UK calcium is added to flour to prevent rickets.

1942 The National Loaf is introduced to combat shortages of white flour
(it resembles modern brown loaves).

1950 Slicing and wrapping of loaves is reintroduced
(having been prohibited during the war for reasons of economy).

1956 The National Loaf is abolished; Mother's Pride becomes a national brand.

1961 A production method developed at the Chorleywood Flour Milling
and Bakery Research Association is introduced, producing the soft,
fluffy loaves familiar ever since.

1969 By now Britons are consuming 42 million sliced white loaves a week.

Hammer horror films starring Peter Cushing and Christopher Lee

1957   *The Curse Of Frankenstein* (PC/CL);
        The Abominable Snowman (PC)

1958   *Dracula* (PC/CL);
        The Revenge Of Frankenstein (PC)

1959   *The Hound Of The Baskervilles* (PC/CL);
        The Mummy (PC/CL);
        The Man Who Could Cheat Death (CL)

1960   *Brides of Dracula* (PC);
        The Two Faces of Dr. Jekyll (CL)

1961   *Taste of Fear* (CL)

1964   *The Evil Of Frankenstein* (PC);
        The Gorgon (PC/CL)

1966   *Dracula: Prince of Darkness* (CL);
        Rasputin, The Mad Monk (CL)

1967   *Frankenstein Created Woman* (PC)

1968   *The Devil Rides Out* (CL);
        Dracula Has Risen From The Grave (CL)

1969   *Frankenstein Must Be Destroyed* (PC)

1970   *Taste the Blood of Dracula* (CL);
        Scars of Dracula (CL);
        The Vampire Lovers (PC)

1971   *Twins of Evil* (PC)

1972   *Dracula AD 1972* (PC/CL)

1974   *The Satanic Rites Of Dracula* (PC/CL);
        Frankenstein and the Monster From Hell (PC);
        The Legend of the 7 Golden Vampires (PC);
        To the Devil a Daughter (CL)

What you needed to be: a Teddy Boy

The name Teddy Boy is said to have been coined by the *Daily Express* and came from the Teddy Boys' choice of Edwardian-style clothes.

Clothes: Drape coats, drainpipe trousers, bootlace ties, waistcoats and winklepicker shoes, or "brothel creepers".

Optional extras: Velvet collars on the drape coats, a watch and chain.

Hairstyles: Highly styled and cultivated quiffs attained with the liberal use of Brylcreem and a "DA" at the back.

Weapons: Flick-knives, bicycle chains and razors (with which to cause trouble while hanging round on street corners, at dances at "The Palais" or just for ripping up cinema seats).

Men's hats

Bowler: Hard, felt hat, usually in black, still worn by city gents in the 1960s.

Fedora: Soft felt hat with a centre crease and pinched in at the sides; perhaps more popular in the USA, although some stylish Brits wore them too.

Flat cap: The classic flat cap worn by working-class factory hands and upper-class huntin', shootin' and fishin' types alike.

Homburg: Similar to a Fedora, but with a fixed shape rather than a malleable one, and a rolled-in brim.

Porkpie: A felt, or sometimes straw, hat with a narrow brim and a flat top.

Trilby: Again similar to the fedora, but with a narrower brim turned up at the back. Famously worn by Frank Sinatra, among others.

1950s hairstyles

The '50s look	Achieved with much pin-curling and rolling. Women often slept with rollers in and there were no blow-dryers to speed the process in the '50s.
The DA	Politely referred to as the "duck's tail", although the "a" may have stood for something else. Greased hair piled high on top, combed back around the sides of the head and parted from the crown to the nape of the neck.
The Gamine	Basically the Audrey Hepburn short-haired, waif-like look.
The crew cut	Essentially the style you got if you went into the military, with hair shaved to an even distance all over the head.
The flat-top	Sides shaved and the top kept longer before being cut in a level plane – hence the flat-top.
The poodle cut	Short style for women with lots of tight curls. Popularized by Lucille Ball.
The bouffant	Hair backcombed with some left hanging at the side. Popularized by Jackie Kennedy.
The ponytail	Favourite style of the bobby-soxers, worn with a poodle skirt and socks rolled down to the ankle.
The beehive	Piled up, teased and lacquered to resemble a beehive balanced on the wearer's head!

People who used to wear uniforms

Cinema commissionaires would wear a full uniform, often with gold-braided jacket, seamed trousers and peaked cap with badge. Ex-army types would complete the outfit with a row of medals on the left breast.

Cinema usherettes in the 1950s and '60s wore smart uniform consisting of skirt and jacket in a colour denoting the cinema that employed them. Pre-1940 they would sometimes wear a knee-length, coat-style uniform over a skirt. They would, of course, also be carrying a small torch. The ladies who sold ice cream and snacks in the interval would wear a different uniform, eg. a pinafore-style dress.

Other cinema workers: even the projectionists would often wear a white laboratory-style coat, while the manager would wear a smart suit.

Park-keepers often wore a blue serge suit and tie, and a peaked cap with braid around it.

School caretakers wore a similar uniform to a park-keeper's, though perhaps with a less military cap.

Wedding superstitions

• On the wedding day, the bride and groom must not meet except at the altar.

• A bride's wedding outfit should include "something old, something new, something borrowed and something blue".

• A bride should never wear her complete wedding outfit before the wedding itself.

• Once married, a bride should be carried over the threshold of her new home by her husband.

Rare foreign stamps that probably never made it to your collection

Mauritius:	One penny and twopence stamps from 1847 mistakenly had the words "post office" instead of "post paid".
Sweden:	An 1855 three-skilling stamp was mistakenly printed on yellow paper instead of green.
USA:	The one cent stamp from 1867 had a "Z grill" pattern which was meant to help the stamp absorb the franking ink, but it was not used on more than a few stamps.
British Guiana:	Emergency issue of stamps when supplies of those from Britain had run out. The pink and black stamps were in one cent and four cent denominations.

Some TV Westerns

Wagon Train Broadcast 1957-65

Starred Ward Bond (as Seth Adams), Robert Horton (Flint McCullough); guest stars included Angie Dickinson, Lou Costello, Peter Lorre, Lee Marvin and Leonard Nimoy.

Gunsmoke Broadcast 1955-75

Starred James Arness (as Matt Dillon), Milburn Stone ("Doc" Adams), Dennis Weaver (limping Chester Goode), Burt Reynolds (Quint Asper), Ken Curtis (Fester McHaggen); was set in Dodge City and opening titles showed Matt Dillon in a gunfight.

Rawhide Broadcast 1959-65

Starred Eric Fleming (as Gil Favor), Clint Eastwood (Rowdy Yates), Sheb Wooley (Pete Nolan); memorable for theme tune ("Rollin', rollin', rollin'...")

Bonanza Broadcast 1959-73

Starred Lorne Greene (as Ben Cartwright), Michael Landon (Little Joe Cartwright), Dan Blocker ("Hoss" Cartwright), Pernell Roberts (Adam Cartwright); memorable for theme tune and opening titles showing map of Ponderosa bursting into flames.

Olympic Games host countries and notable events

1948: London	The "Flying Housewife", Fanny Blankers-Koen of the Netherlands, won four gold medals in 100 metres, 200 metres, 80 metre high hurdles, and 4 x 100 metres relay.
1952: Helsinki	Hungary, with a population of just 9,000,000, won 42 medals. The USSR and Israel each competed for the first time.
1956: Melbourne and Stockholm	The main games were held in Melbourne, but due to quarantine restrictions the equestrian events could not be held in Australia and instead were held in Sweden.
1960: Rome	The gold medal for the boxing light-heavyweight event was won by Cassius Clay (later Muhammed Ali).
1964: Tokyo	This was the first Olympics at which fibreglass poles were used for vaulting.
1968: Mexico	Americans Tommie Smith and John Carlos famously raised their fists in Black Power salutes during the 200 metres awards ceremony.
1972: Munich	Palestinian guerrillas belonging to the Black September organization took eleven Israeli athletes, coaches and officials hostage and two were killed.
1976: Montreal	At the opening ceremony, the Israeli national flag bore a black ribbon in memory of the 1972 Munich massacre.

1950s lingerie

Seamed stockings • suspenders or elastic roll-on • corset • girdle
cantilever bra • chilly gap on thigh where stockings ended

Snap, crackle and pop (Rice Krispies).

It's smart to start with Kellogg's Corn Flakes.

Un-zipp (sic) a banana!

Oxo gives a meal man appeal.

Go to work on an egg (the Egg Marketing Board).

I'm a happy knocker-upper
　　And I'm popular beside
　　'Cos I wake 'em with a cuppa
　　And tasty Mother's Pride. (TV ad sung by Dusty Springfield)

Milk's gotta lotta bottle.

Don't say "brown", say "Hovis".

Don't say "gravy", say "Bisto"! Ahh, Bisto!

Don't say "K-norr", say "kNorr"!

Mighty meaty, matey (Dring's sausages).

Nimble – real bread, but lighter.

Graded grains make finer flour (Homepride).

For mash, get Smash!

Mr Kipling makes exceedingly good cakes.

Can you tell Stork from butter?

Nice one, Cyril/Nice one, son/
　　Nice one, Cyril, let's have another one (Wonderloaf).

Good morning, good morning, the best to you each morning.
(Kellogg's Corn Flakes).

We like Ricicles, they're twicicles as nicicles,
We like Ricicles, they're twicicles as nice

Tell 'em about the honey, mummy (Sugar Puffs).

Central heating for kids (Ready Brek).

No wonder Weetabix is unbeatabix.

Mother's Pride's a family – a family of bread.

A million housewives every day/ pick up a can of beans and say/
"Beanz meanz Heinz!"

Don't be mean with the beans, mum! Beanz meanz Heinz!

Ski – the full of fitness food!

1950s 3D movies

Title	Year of release	Stars
Bwana Devil (The first 3D film)	1952	Robert Stack and Barbara Britton
House of Wax	1953	Vincent Price
Kiss Me, Kate	1953	Kathryn Grayson and Howard Kee
Hondo	1953	John Wayne
Man in the Dark	1953	Edmund O'Brien and Audrey Totte
Melody	1953	Walt Disney (**The first 3D cartoon)**
It Came From Outer Space	1953	Richard Carlson and Barbara Rush
Robot Monster	1953	George Nader and Claudia Barrett
Inferno	1953	Robert Ryan and Rhonda Fleming
Top Banana	1954	Phil Silvers
The French Line	1954	Jane Russell
Taza, Son of Cochise	1954	Rock Hudson
Phantom of the Rue Morgue	1954	Karl Malden
Gorilla at Large	1954	Cameron Mitchell
Creature From the Black Lagoon	1954	Richard Carlson and Julie Adams
House on Haunted Hill	1959	Vincent Price and Carol Ohmart
The Tingler	1959	Vincent Price

George Orwell's six rules of writing

In his 1946 essay "Politics and the English Language", George Orwell offered the following advice for writers:

- Writers should never use metaphors, similes and other figures of speech which are often seen in print.

- A long word should not be used if there is an appropriate short alternative.

- If a word can be cut out, then it should be cut out.

- Writers should not use the passive if they can use the active.

- English equivalents should be used whenever possible instead of foreign phrases, scientific words or jargon.

- Orwell's final rule was however, "Break any of these rules sooner than say anything outright barbarous."

Polygons

A regular polygon = one in which all the sides are equal.

Every time you add an extra side to a polygon, it adds 180° to the total of all the angles. To work out the angles in a regular polygon, divide the total of all the angles by the number of sides. So:

Polygon	No of sides	Total number of degrees	Size each angle in regular polygon
Triangle	3	180	60
Quadrilateral	4	360	90
Pentagon	5	540	108
Hexagon	6	720	120
Heptagon	7	900	128.57
Octagon	8	1,080	135
Nonagon	9	1,260	140
Decagon	10	1,440	144
Undecagon or Hendecagon	11	1,620	147.27
Dodecagon	12	1,800	150
Triskaidecagon	13	1,980	152.31
Tetrakaidecagon	14	2,160	154.29
Pendedecagon	15	2,340	156
Hexdecagon	16	2,520	157.5
Heptdecagon	17	2,700	158.82
Octdecagon	18	2,880	160
Enneadecagon	19	3,060	161.05
Icosagon	20	3,240	162
Triacontagon	30	5,040	168
Tetracontagon	40	6,840	171

Developments designated by the New Towns Act 1946

Crawley, Sussex • Bracknell, Berkshire • Harlow, Essex • Basildon, Essex • Hatfield, Hertfordshire • Hemel Hempstead, Hertfordshire • Stevenage, Hertfordshire • Corby, Northamptonshire • Cwmbran, Monmouthshire • Peterlee, County Durham • Glenrothes, Fife • Newton Aycliffe, County Durham • East Kilbride, Lanarkshire • Welwyn Garden City (extension), Hertfordshire

Items added to the list of goods used to assess the cost of living

In order to calculate changes in the cost of living, the Office of National Statistics uses the prices of a range of popular goods. But what items have been added to the list at different periods over the past 65 years?

1947: Bicycles, cinema tickets, corned beef, electricity, football tickets, gramophone records, radios, sewing machines.

1950s: Canned fruit, cars, dance hall and youth club admission charges, ice cream, motorcycle insurance, NHS prescription charges, photographic film, Tupperware, television sets.

1960s: Fish fingers, girdles, jeans, paper tissues, refrigerators, restaurant meals, scooters, sherry, sliced white bread.

1970s: Aluminium foil, bingo fees, cassette recorders, duvets, electric hairdryers, home perm kits, mortgage interest payments, record players, wine, yoghurt.

1980s: Compact discs, condoms, frozen ready meals, low-alcohol lager, microwave ovens, telephones, video recorders, videotapes.

1990s: Aerobic class fees, CD-ROMs, computer games, foreign holidays, Internet charges, leggings, multivitamins, private education, replica football strips, satellite dishes.

Advertising slogans from our youth: fuel

- Blue, blue, blue, blue, blue, blue, blue, Esso Blue...
- The Esso sign means happy motoring, happy motoring, the Esso sign means happy motoring, so call at the Esso sign – for Esso Extra!
- Keep going well, keep going Shell, you can be sure of Shell.
- I'm going well, I'm going Shell, I'm going well on Shell, Shell, Shell (TV ad sung by Bing Crosby).
- Put a tiger in your tank! (Esso).

Makes of cars launched by year

1946	Renault 4CV/ Triumph Roadster/ Wolseley 8.
1947	Austin Princess/ Austin A40 Countryman/ Peugeot 203.
1948	Citroen 2CV/ Jaguar XK120/ Land Rover/ Morris Minor.
1949	Ford Anglia E494A/ Rover P4.
1950	Aston Martin DB2/ Ford Zephyr/ Fiat 1400.
1951	Ford Consul/ Jaguar C Type.
1953	Austin Healey 100/ Ford Anglia 100E/ Ford Popular 103E / Isetta and Messerschmitt KR175 bubblecars/ Reliant Regal / Riley Pathfinder/ Sunbeam Alpine/ Triumph TR2.
1954	Austin Cambridge A40 and A50/ Hillman Husky/ Vauxhall Cresta.
1955	Citroen DS/ Fiat 600/ Jaguar Mark 1/ Peugeot 403/ Rolls-Royce Silver Cloud/ Sunbeam Rapier/ Triumph TR3.
1956	Austin A35/ Citroen ID19/ Jaguar Mark VIII.
1957	Austin Cambridge A55/ Fiat 500/ Lotus Elite/ Morris Marshal / Riley One-Point-Five/ Vauxhall Victor/ Wolseley 1500.
1958	Aston Martin DB4/ Austin A40 Farina/ Morris Major/ Rover P5 / Wolseley 15/60.
1959	Austin-Healey 3000/ Fiat 1800/2100/ Ford Anglia 105E / Ford Popular 100E/ The Mini, aka the Morris Mini-Minor/ Riley 4.
1960	Peugeot 404.
1961	Austin Cambridge A60/ Hillman Superminx/Jaguar E Type / MG Midget/ Renault 4/ Riley Elf.
1962	Ford Cortina/ Morris 1100/ Triumph Spitfire.
1963	Hillman Imp/ Rover P6/ Triumph 2000/ Vauxhall Viva.
1964	Fiat 850/ Reliant Rebel/ Sunbeam Tiger.
1965	Ford Transit/ Triumph 1300.
1966	Fiat 124/ Jensen Interceptor/ Nissan Sunny/ Toyota Corolla / Triumph GT6.
1967	Audi 80/ Fiat 125/ Ford Escort.
1968	Audi 100/ Datsun 510/Jaguar XJ/ Peugeot 504.
1969	Austin Maxi/ Ford Capri/ Peugeot 304.
1970	Hillman Avenger/ Nissan Cherry/ Range Rover/ Triumph Stag.
1971	Morris Marina/ Peugeot 104/ Renault 5.
1972	Triumph Dolomite.
1973	Austin Allegro/ Honda Civic/ Volkswagen Passat.
1974	Renault 7/ Volkswagen Golf.

Children's TV series starting by year

1946 *Muffin the Mule.*
1955 *Crackerjack; The Sooty Show.*
1956 *Lassie.*
1957 *The Adventures of Twizzle; Captain Pugwash; Pinky and Perky.*
1958 *Blue Peter.*
1959 *Ivor the Engine; Noggin the Nog.*
1960 *Four Feather Falls.*
1961 *Supercar.*
1962 *Animal Magic; Fireball XL5; Hergé's Adventures of Tintin.*
1963 *Doctor Who.*
1964 *Play School; Stingray.*
1965 *Jackanory; The Magic Roundabout; Thunderbirds.*
1966 *Daktari; Flipper; How.*
1967 *The Adventures Of Robinson Crusoe; Belle and Sebastian;*
    Captain Scarlet and The Mysterons; Skippy.
1968 *Hector's House; Joe 90; Magpie; The White Horses.*
1969 *Clangers.*
1970 *Catweazle; Here Come the Double Deckers; Timeslip; UFO.*
1971 *Follyfoot; Mr Benn.*
1972 *The Adventures Of Black Beauty; Crystal Tipps and Alistair;*
    Record Breakers.
1973 *Pipkins; The Tomorrow People; Why Don't You Just Switch Off Your*
    Television Set and Go and Do Something Less Boring Instead?
1974 *Bagpuss; Roobarb; Tiswas.*
1975 *Runaround; Paddington Bear.*
1976 *Multi-Coloured Swap Shop.*
1978 *Grange Hill.*

For foreign series, starting dates shown are for first broadcast in UK.

Some memorable strikes

1968: Ford machinists at Dagenham.
1970-71: ITN workers' "colour strike".
1971: Post Office workers' strike.
1972: Miners' strike.
1974: Miners' strike.
1976-77: Grunwick film processing laboratories, Willesden, London; workers
went on strike demanding union recognition.
1978-79: "Winter of Discontent".

Dance crazes popularized by hit records

Dance	Record
Hand Jive	"Willie And The Hand Jive" by Johnny Otis (1958)
Hully Gully	"(Baby) Hully Gully" by The Olympics (1959)
The Twist	"The Twist" by Chubby Checker (1960)
	which he followed up with "Let's Twist Again" (1962)
The Mashed Potato	"Mashed Potato Time" by Dee Dee Sharpe (1962).
	Also mentioned in "Do You Love Me" by The Contours
	and "Let's Dance" by Chris Montez
The Hitch Hike	"Hitch Hike" by Marvin Gaye (1962)
The Loco-motion	"The Loco-motion" by Little Eva (1962)
The Monkey	"The Monkey Time" by Major Lance
	and "Mickey's Monkey" by The Miracles (1963)
The Swim	"C'mon And Swim" by Bobby Freeman (1964)
The Funky Chicken	"Do The Funky Chicken" by Rufus Thomas (1970)

UK Toy Retailers' Association most popular toys of the 1960s

1960	Lego.
1961	Airfix Betta Bilda sets (10s each).
	Chad Valley Give-A-Show projector.
1962	The Pogo stick.
1963	Matchbox cars with opening doors.
1964	Trolls.
1965	Gonks.
	Spirograph.
1966	Action Man. Tiny Tears.
	Tommy Gunn (Pedigree's answer to Action Man).
	Twister.
1967	Etch-a-Sketch.
	Johnny Astro with astronaut, launch pad,
	moon surface and three space vehicles.
1968	Sindy. Go Car game
	(involving a breathalyzer test hazard!).
	Glow-in-the dark modelling clay Glow-Globs.
	Paintwheels.
1969	Hot Wheels cars.
	Newton's Cradle (Klikkies).

Advertising slogans from our youth: cleaning

- Now hands that do dishes can feel soft as your face with mild green Fairy Liquid.

- Fairy Snow gives washday white without washday red.

- White Tide – not only clean, but deep-down clean.

- Hold it up to the light: not a stain and shining bright (Surf).

- Domestos kills all known germs – dead!

- Ajax – cleans like a white tornado.

- There's a softness and a freshness you've never known before that's the loving touch of New Lenor!

- Dainty things never shrink from Lux!

- Persil washes whiter — and it shows!

- The cleanest clean under the sun is Tide clean.

- Ten thousand flies killed – fast as this. It's Vapona. A fly killer you can trust!

- Ring around the collar (Wisk detergent).

- Fairy's a must for collars and cuffs! (Fairy household soap).

- Forces grey out, forces white in (Fairy Snow).

- Flash cuts cleaning time in half.

- 1001 cleans a big, big carpet for less than half a crown.

- A brighter carpet means a brighter home, 1001 Dry Foam.

- Harpic – cleans right around the bend.

- Ariel – The dirt says "hot", the label says "not".

- Fairy Snow – it gets right to the heart of the wash.

- Have Liquid Dreft on hand … in case the handmaidens call!

- Omo adds brightness to whiteness.

- Omo – so bright even a man notices!

- Softness is a thing called Comfort!

- It's so easy with Sqezy!

- Cleans and polishes in one go! (Pledge furniture polish).

Playground games

What's the time, Mr Wolf?

One person is elected "wolf" and stands with their back to the rest of the group. The group asks in unison "What's the time, Mr Wolf?" and the wolf replies with any time of his choosing. If he says "one o'clock" the group moves one step towards him; if he says "two o'clock" then they move two steps forward and so on. Then, whenever he chooses, the wolf can suddenly reply "Dinner time!" and chase and catch members of the group.

It, or He

One person is designated as "it" and has to count to an agreed number before chasing the other children. If they catch them then that person is "it", and has to chase and catch one of the others.

He ball

Similar to the above game but instead of catching other people you have to hit them with the ball.

Fag cards

Players take turns to flick cigarette cards on to the ground. When your card lands on top of another one you win all the cards that are on the ground.

Lolly sticks

One player holds a lolly stick horizontally by the ends. The other player swipes their lolly stick down in a chopping motion with the object of breaking the other player's stick in half. Players take turns until one stick is completely chopped in half.

Dolls for boys and girls

Action Man   Introduced in 1966, licensed from Hasbro by Palitoy.
First came out in three uniforms: Army, Navy and Air Force.
Hair colours varied from blond to brown, to auburn or black.

Tommy Gunn   British version of the American-inspired Action Man,
dressed as a British infantryman carrying a Sterling
sub-machine gun; a later version wore a World War Two
uniform and carried a Sten gun.

Barbie   Produced by Mattel in 1959; the first Barbie wore a black
and white zebra-striped swimming costume. Choice of hair
colour was blonde or brunette. First advertised as a "teen-age
fashion model". In 1971 Barbie dolls began to be made with
her eyes looking to the front rather than sideways, as before.

Sindy   Launched in 1963 by Pedigree Dolls and Toys, Sindy was
sold as "The doll you love to dress", a slogan borrowed with
permission from the US manufacturers of Tammy, which had
been produced in 1962. In 1965 Sindy acquired a boyfriend
named Paul, the following year a younger sister named
Patch; in 1968 Sindy also acquired a couple of friends, Vicki
and Mitzi, and Patch had new playmates Poppet and Betsy.

Some toys that are older than you think...

- Yo-yo – thought to have been around since 500BC!
  There was a craze for them in 1929, then again in the early 1960s.

- Roller skates – people have been falling over on these since 1759.

- Kewpie Dolls – first manufactured by German company J D Kestner
  in 1913, based on the comic-strip creations of American illustrator
  Rose O'Neill. The name "Kewpie" came from Cupid.

- Clackers – the balls on a string which you clacked together were a craze
  around 1970. The first UK patent was, however, as early as 1949.

Derby winners and riders

Year	Horse	Jockey	Trainer
1950	Galcador	W Johnstone	Charles Semblat
1951	Arctic Prince	C Spares	Willie Stephenson
1952	Tulyar	C Smirke	Marcus Marsh
1953	Pinza	G Richards	Norman Bertie
1954	Never Say Die	L Piggott	Joe Lawson
1955	Phil Drake	F Palmer	François Mathet
1956	Lavandin	W Johnstone	Alec Head
1957	Crepello	L Piggott	Noel Murless
1958	Hard Ridden	C Smirke	Mick Rogers
1959	Parthia	W H Carr	Captain Cecil Boyd-Rochfort
1960	St Paddy	L Piggott	Noel Murless
1961	Psidium	R Poincelet	R. Poincelet
1962	Larkspur	N Sellwood	Vincent O'Brien
1963	Relko	Y Saint-Martin	Francois Mathet
1964	Santa Claus	A Beasley	Mick Rogers
1965	Sea Bird II	T P Glennon	Etienne Pollet
1966	Charlottown	A Beasley	Gordon Smyth
1967	Royal Palace	G Moore	Noel Murless
1968	Sir Ivor	L Piggott	Vincent O'Brien
1969	Blakeney	E Johnson	Mr A M Budgett

Popes since 1945

Pope	Name before becoming Pope	Nat'y	In office
Pius XII	Eugenio Maria Giuseppe Giovanni Pacelli	Italian	1939-58
John XXIII	Angelo Giuseppe Roncalli	Italian	1958-63
Paul VI	Giovanni Battista Enrico Antonio Maria Montini	Italian	1963-78
John Paul I	Albino Luciani	Italian	26/08/1978 - 28/09/1978
John Paul II	Karol Józef Wojtyla	Polish	1978-2005
Benedict XVI	Joseph Aloisius Ratzinger	German	2005-

Armed forces ranks

British Army	Royal Navy	Royal Air Force
Field Marshal	Admiral of the Fleet	Marshal of the Royal Air Force
General	Admiral	Air Chief Marshal
Lieutenant General	Vice-Admiral	Air Marshal
Major-General	Rear-Admiral	Air Vice-Marshal
Brigadier	Commodore	Air Commodore
Colonel	Captain	Group Captain
Lieutenant Colonel	Commander	Wing Commander
Major	Lieutenant Commander	Squadron Leader
Captain	Lieutenant	Flight Lieutenant
Lieutenant	Sub-Lieutenant	Flying Officer
2nd Lieutenant	Midshipman	Pilot Officer
Warrant Officer 1st Class (Regimental Sergeant Major)	Warrant Officer 1	Warrant Officer 1
Warrant Officer 2nd Class (Company/Squadron Sergeant Major)	Warrant Officer 2	Warrant Officer 2
Staff/ Colour Sergeant	Chief Petty Officer	Flight Sergeant/ Chief Technician
Sergeant	Petty Officer	Sergeant
Corporal	Leading Seaman	Corporal
Lance Corporal		Senior Aircraftman/ Junior Technician
Private (Gunner in the Royal Artillery; Sapper in the Royal Engineers; Signaller in the Royal Signals; Trooper in the cavalry; Craftsman in the Royal Electrical and Mechanical Engineers).	Able Seaman	Aircraftman

Ways to cheat at Conkers

*Of course, no self-respecting wrinkly would dream of such a thing,
but these were some of the underhand tricks used by others back in the day:*

- Soaking them in vinegar. It was thought that thus pickling your weapon of choice would toughen it up and render it unbreakable. Legends of 101-ers abound.

- Baking them in the oven. A couple of hours at gas mark 6 would turn your sappy horse chestnut into the conker equivalent of a silver bullet: unless, of course, your mum caught you, or the shilling in the gas meter ran out.

- Varnishing them. Using your big sister's best nail varnish to toughen up your conker was dangerous in so many ways...

- Keeping them for a year. Stashing a few conkers away at the back of the shoe cupboard meant that when they re-emerged next season they were fearsome fighting machines. Giveaway signs: a darker than usual hue and a strong smell of old boots.

- Cutting them in half and concealing a stone in the middle. Absolutely filthy tactics and only countenanced by the most underhand of players. They would, of course, be found out when the conker casing split to reveal an unconkerlike lump of granite dangling from your string.

- Pulling your conker away just as your opponent took their shot. Not only did your opponent miss hitting your conker, but there was a fair chance their own conker would complete a full circle and bash them in the eye.

- Using elastic instead of string. The moveability of your conker would mean that the impact of your opponent's weapon would be minimized. Downside; your own conker could well bounce back and hit you in the eye – which would probably serve you right!

Commemorative stamp issues

1940: Centenary of the first adhesive postage stamps. Design showed Queen Victoria and King George VI.

1946: Victory stamps showed images of peace and reconstruction.

1948: Royal Silver wedding issue commemorated marriage of Prince Albert, Duke of York, and Lady Elizabeth Bowes-Lyons (King George VI and Queen Elizabeth).

1948: London Olympics set of four stamps showed images of speed and victory.

1949: 75th anniversary of the Postal Union: four stamps in same colours as Olympics set above (brown, blue, lilac and mauve).

1951: Festival of Britain: red and blue stamps showing Britannia and a cornucopia.

1953: Coronation: set of four at tuppence ha'penny, fourpence, one shilling and threepence and one shilling and sixpence.

1957: World Scout Jubilee Jamboree: a set of three in red, blue and green, showing Scouting symbol, globe etc.

1957: 46th Inter-Parliamentary Union conference: single blue 4d stamp.

1958: Sixth British Empire and Commonwealth Games.

1960: Tercentenary of Establishment of General Letter Office.

1960: First anniversary of European Postal and Telecommunications Conference.

Historic space flights pre-Apollo

October 4, 1957: *Sputnik* launched by USSR

November 3, 1957: *Sputnik 2* launched by USSR carrying Laika ("Barker"), a stray dog that had been found on the streets of Moscow.

January 31, 1958: *Explorer 1* launched by USA.

October 1, 1958: Foundation of NASA.

January 2, 1959: *Luna 1*, launched by USSR, orbits the moon.

March 3, 1959: *Pioneer 4* launched by USA and goes on to pass within 37,000 miles of the Moon before orbiting around the sun.

September 13, 1959: A day after its launch by the USSR, *Luna 2* becomes the first man-made object to hit the Moon.

October 4, 1959: USSR launches *Luna 3* which orbits the Moon, photographing 70% of its dark side.

April 12, 1961: USSR launches *Vostok 1* carrying Yuri Gargarin, who orbits the Earth once, in 108 minutes.

May 5, 1961: USA launches Mercury capsule *Freedom 7*, piloted by Alan Shepard, on a 15-minute sub-orbital flight.

August 6, 1961: USSR launches *Vostok 2*, carrying Gherman Titov on the first day-long space flight.

February 20, 1962: USA launches Mercury capsule *Friendship 7* piloted by John Glenn, who orbits the Earth three times in a flight lasting nearly five hours.

July 10, 1962: USA launches the Telstar communication satellite, which relayed the first TV pictures through space including the first transatlantic live TV feed.

Decemebr 14, 1962: The USA's *Mariner 2* flies past Venus before going into orbit around the sun.

June 16, 1963: The USSR's Valentia Tereshkova becomes the first woman in space and orbits the Earth 48 times on board *Vostok 6*.

March 18, 1965: The USSR's Alexei A. Leonov makes the first space walk, from *Voskhod 2*.

June 3, 1965: The USA's Edward White makes a 22-minute space walk from *Gemini 4*.

November 16, 1965: USSR launches *Venus 3*, which impacts on Venus in March 1966.

December 4, 1965: *Gemini 7* is launched, carrying Frank Borman and Jim Lovell; it makes 206 orbits of the Earth and demonstrates the possibility of a trip to the Moon.

February 3, 1966: The Soviet *Luna 9* is the first craft to soft-land on the Moon.

Doctor Who

The first nine actors to play the Doctor:

William Hartnell	November 23, 1963-October 29, 1966 (plus guest appearance in *The Three Doctors* December 30, 1972-January 20, 1973).
Peter Cushing	In films *Doctor Who And The Daleks* (1965) and *The Daleks Invasion Earth 2150 AD* (1966).
Patrick Troughton	October 29, 1966-June 21, 1969 (plus guest appearances in "The Three Doctors", December 30, 1972-January 20, 1973; "The Five Doctors", November 23, 1983; and "The Two Doctors", February16-March 2, 1985).
Jon Pertwee	January 3, 1970-June 8, 1974 (plus guest appearance in "The Five Doctors", November 23, 1983).
Tom Baker	June 8, 1974-March 21, 1981.
Peter Davison	March 21, 1981-March 16, 1984.
Richard Hurndall	Guest appearance in "The Five Doctors", November 23, 1983.
Colin Baker	March 16, 1984-December 6, 1986.
Sylvester McCoy	September 7, 1987-May 27, 1989.

Actors who have played the Doctor in order of date of birth:

William Hartnell	(1908-75)
Richard Hurndall	(1910-84)
Peter Cushing	(1913-94)
Jon Pertwee	(1919-96)
Patrick Troughton	(1920-87)
Tom Baker	(born 1934)
Colin Baker	(born 1943)
Sylvester McCoy	(born 1943)
Peter Davison	(born 1951)
Paul McGann	(born 1959)
Christopher Ecclestone	(born 1964)
David Tennant	(born 1971)
Matt Smith	(born 1982)

Social entertainments
in more innocent days

Dinner and dance

Before we had quite so many restaurants to choose from, it was common in the 1950s and '60s for mum and dad to dress up and go to a dinner and dance in the local church hall; these often ended up with people dancing the conga out of the church hall door, round the car park and back in again.

Whist drives

This card game for four people was turned into a social event by the whist drive, at which people could play through various heats.

Beetle drives

Assembling a plastic beetle piece by piece depending on the roll of dice may seem an odd thing for adults to do on a Saturday night, but these drives too were popular in the 1950s and '60s.

Bingo/Housey Housey/Lotto

All one and the same game, and often played in church halls before the advent of commercial bingo halls from 1961 onwards.

Church youth clubs

Before teenage binge-drinking, computer games and other modern diversions, young teenagers would often go to the local youth club, usually held in a church hall, where there would be a Dansette record player, table tennis and perhaps a few jugs of squash and maybe even a few nibbles if you were lucky.

Other comics

Comic	Date of first issue	Strips included
The Rover	March 4, 1922	Alf Tupper, Nosey Parker, Morgyn the Mighty, Telegraph Tim, The Wonder Man, Thick-Ear Donovan, The Robot Boy, Pony Express, V For Vengeance, The Barrow Boy From Mars, I Flew With Braddock, It's Goals That Count.
The Wizard	September 22, 1922	Cool Cassidy, Red Macgregor, Georgeous Gus, Red Star Roberts, Magnus the Muscle Man, Thruster John, The Circus of Sudden Death, Wilson the Wonder Athlete, The Wolf of Kabul (with his sidekick Chung and his cricket bat weapon "clicky ba"), Limp-Along Leslie who played football for Darbury Rangers.
The Hotspur	September 2, 1933 (became The New Hotspur from October 24, 1959, and then just The Hotspur again from February 16, 1963)	Cannonball Kid, Captain Zoom, Charlie The Kettle, Hoppy The Hobo, The Iron Teacher, The Smasher, Sammy The Fearless Funk, The Terrible Quests Of Blind Mcgraw, Tongue-Twisting Champion Of Britain, Tommy Gunn And Trigger, Red Circle School (with bully Alfred Smug), Silas Snatcher, Truant Catcher, and Union Jack Jackson.
The Eagle	April 14, 1950	Dan Dare – Pilot of the Future, Harris Tweed – Special Agent, PC49, Waldorf and Cecil, Luck of the Legion, Jack O'Lantern, Tommy Walls, Storm Nelson, Riders of the Range.
The Beezer	January 21, 1956	Baby Crockett, The Badd Lads, Ginger, Colonel Blink – the Short-Sighted Gink, Smiffy, Pop Dick and Harry, Nosey Parker, Nero And Zero, Calamity Jane, The Banana Bunch, The Hillys and the Billys, Big Ed the Heavyweight Chump, Young Sid the Copper's Kid.
The Topper	February 7, 1953	Micky the Monkey, Beryl the Peril, King Gussie, Julius Cheeser, Desert Island Dick, Big Fat Boko, Circus of Fear, Flip McCoy, Jiffy and the Glyphs, Captain Bungle, Jimmy's Magic Midgets.
The Victor	January 25, 1961	Alf Tupper, Tough of The Track, Morgyn the Mighty, Joe Bones, The Human Fly, The Goals of Jimmy Grant.

Mods and rockers

Details	Mods	Rockers
Style of dress	Parkas, Levi jeans, loafers, Italian-cut mohair suits, tab-collar shirts.	Leather jackets, jeans, boots.
Mode of transport	Scooter (Lambretta or Vespa) – preferably adorned with lots of mirrors and lights.	Motorbike – preferably British, such as Triumph or Norton or their hybrid, the Triton.
Hairstyle	Short, neat, centre parting, backcombed on top.	Quiff held in place by Brylcreem.
Music	Soul, Tamla Motown, Blue Beat, The Who, Kinks, Small Faces, Yardbirds etc.	1950s rock 'n' roll.
Demeanour	Cool, detached.	Rough and moody.
Places seen	Carnaby Street, trendy clubs.	Bikers cafés, dancehalls.
Height of fame	Fighting with rockers on Brighton Beach, 1964.	Fighting with Mods on Brighton Beach, 1964.
Ultimate role model	Steve Marriott circa 1965.	Marlon Brando circa 1953.
Interests	Clothes, music, dancing.	Motorbikes, punch-ups.
Style of dance	Cool, minimal movement.	The famous "shoulder dance".

The first teddy bear

The teddy bear, surely, has been around for ever – no childhood could possibly be complete without one – but in fact teddies only go back to the early 1900s; though there had been stuffed toy bears before, they were lifelike, fierce and on all fours. The name comes from American president Theodore "Teddy" Roosevelt, an avid hunter. On a trip to Mississippi in November 1902 to sort out a border dispute with Louisiana, his hosts took him hunting; bears were few and eventually he was invited to shoot a captured adult tied to a tree. He refused, deeming it unsporting, though he insisted the bear should be killed to end its suffering. The incident inspired a political cartoon by Clifford Berryman in the Washington Post, "Drawing the Line in Mississippi", showing an adult bear; later versions turned it into a cute cub. Seeing this image, Morris and Rose Michtom, New York sweetshop owners who made soft toys as a sideline, created a stuffed bear cub and put it in their window labelled "Teddy's Bear", having first sent one to the President and received permission to use his name. The bears sold well; the Michtoms founded a company producing them and the craze guaranteed a strong market for the stuffed bears being imported into the US from the Steiff firm in Germany – which had coincidentally begun making them at the same time, inspired by Richard Steiff's studies of bear cubs in the Stuttgart Zoo. By 1906 the craze had taken such a hold that fashionable women carried the bears as accessories and Roosevelt used one in his re-election campaign.

Eating out: Berni Inns

This chain of restaurants started in 1955 and was still around until the late 1990s, though their heyday was probably the 1960s and '70s.

Sample menu:

First course	Second course	Pudding
Melon boat with maraschino cherry	Steak	Black Forest gâteau
Prawn cocktail	Gammon steak	Irish coffee
	Plaice with chips and peas	After Eight mints

Radio 1

The first broadcast on Radio 1 was the Tony Blackburn show starting at 7am on Saturday, September 30, 1967. The first piece of music played on the station was "Theme One" by George Martin, while the songs played on the first show were:

"Beefeaters"	John Dankworth, **the show's theme tune.**
"Homburg"	Procol Harum.
"Flowers in The Rain"	The Move.
"You Keep Running Away"	The Four Tops.
"Massachusetts"	The Bee Gees.
"Let's Go to San Francisco"	The Flower Pot Men.
"Even the Bad Times are Good"	The Tremeloes.
"Handy Man"	Jimmy James.
"Fakin' It"	Simon and Garfunkel.
"You Know What I Mean"	The Turtles.
"The Day I Met Marie"	Cliff Richard.
"The House That Jack Built"	The Alan Price Set.
"You Can't Hurry Love"	The Supremes.
"Excerpt From a Teenage Opera"	Keith West.
"The Last Waltz"	Engelbert Humperdinck.
"Reflections"	Diana Ross and the Supremes.
"Baby Now That I've Found You"	The Foundations.
"King Midas in Reverse"	The Hollies.
"Good Times"	Eric Burdon and the Animals.
"Ode to Billy Joe"	Bobby Gentry.
"A Banda"	Herb Alpert and the Tijuana Brass.
"Then He Kissed Me"	The Crystals.
"I Feel Love Comin' On"	Felice Taylor.
"Anything Goes"	Harpers Bizarre.
"How Can I Be Sure"	Young Rascals.
"The Letter"	The Box Tops.
"Major to Minor"	The Settlers.
"Beefeaters"	John Dankworth.

Party games

Pin the tail on the donkey

Pin a picture of a donkey without a tail to the wall. Blindfold, the contestants try one by one to pin the tail on in the correct place.

Blind man's buff

One person is blindfolded and spun round several times to disorientate them. Everyone else hides and the "blind man" has to find them.

Postman's knock

One person is designated "postman" and has to go out of the room and knock on the door. Someone is then chosen to answer the door and "pay" for the letter with a kiss.

Squeak, piggy, squeak

One person is blindfolded and spun round while everyone else finds a seat. The blindfolded person then has to sit on the lap of one of the participants and say, "Squeak, piggy, squeak". If the blindfolded person correctly identifies the person they are sitting on from the sound of their squeak, the identified person is blindfolded and the game starts again.

Simon says

One person gives the rest of the group instructions to perform tasks, such as holding up right hand, sitting down, scratching head etc. They have to follow each instruction if it is preceded by "Simon Says", but not if it doesn't. If they break this rule they are out.

First stores opened by well-known high-street names

Store	Date	Store location
W H Smith (newsvendors)	1792	Little Grosvenor Street, London
Debenhams	1813	Wigmore Street, London
W H Smith (book stall)	1848	Euston Station, London
Timothy Whites	1848	Portsmouth
Boots	1849	Goose Gate, Nottingham
John Lewis	1864	Oxford Street, London
Liberty	1875	Regent Street, London
Marks and Spencer	1894	Cheetham Hill Road, Manchester
F W Woolworth	1909	Church Street, Liverpool
Selfridges	1909	Oxford Street, London
C&A	1922	Oxford Street, London

1960s pop magazines

Fabulous
Glossy full-colour magazine which started in 1964 and which was full of pin-ups of '60s beat groups and heartthrobs such as Richard Chamberlain (Dr Kildare) and footballer George Best. Cost in 1964: 1s.

Melody Maker
Black and white newspaper-style pop weekly which still featured a lot of jazz in the 1950s but had to give way to pop with the arrival of the Beatles. Cost in 1964: 9d.

Mirabelle
Colour cover, black and white inside with strip-cartoon love stories, pop features, fashion and beauty tips. Cost in 1964: 6d.

New Musical Express
Another black and white newspaper-style weekly that concentrated more on the pop end of the market in the '60s and moved into rock in the '70s. Cost in 1964: 6d.

Rave
A slightly more grown-up version of Fabulous – "The frank look at today's pop world" – containing pin-ups, interviews, film and gig guides. Price in 1964: a whopping 2s 6d!

Also available:

Beat Instrumental; Disc and Music Echo; Flexipop; Jackie; Just 17; Marty; Merseybeat; Pop Pics; Record Mirror; Rolling Stone; Roxy; Superpop; Valentine; Zigzag...

Some London nightclubs
of the Swinging Sixties

- Annabel's • The Cromwellian • Bag Of Nails • Pickwick • Tramps •
- Sybilla's • Esmeralda's Barn • Scotch of St James's • Speakeasy •
- Flamingo • Whiskey a Go Go • The Scene • The Establishment •

Round the Horne

Round the Horne was a radio comedy series broadcast between 1965 and 1968 on the Light Programme and then Radio 2. Kenneth Horne was the star of the show and the other performers were:

Kenneth Williams	Rambling Syd Rumpo *("I'll sing you one-oh, green grow my nadgers-oh!")*; Sandy *(Julian's friend – "How bona to vada your jolly old eek")*; Dr Chou En Ginsberg *(Oriental criminal mastermind- "Ah, Mr Horne! We meet again!")*; J Peasemold Gruntfuttock *(the world's dirtiest old man)*.
Hugh Paddick	Julian *(Sandy's friend)*; Lotus Blossom *(Dr Chou En Ginsberg's strangely gruff-voiced concubine)*; Binkie Huckabuck *(ageing juvenile thespian)*.
Betty Marsden	Dame Celia Molestrangler; Fanny Haddock; Daphne Whitethigh *(hoarse-voiced fashion expert)*.
Bill Pertwee	Seamus Android *(Unskilled television labourer - "Ha-ha; alright. Now then – er… ha- ha – well, that's enough of me")*.

Some fondly-remembered tipples

Gin and it   Sophisticated cocktail of the 1960s: Italian sweet vermouth mixed with gin and ice.

Lager top   Three-quarters of a pint of lager made up to a pint with lemonade. Well, no self-respecting skinhead would have ordered a shandy!

Rum 'n' black   A dash of blackcurrant could perhaps fool young Mod girls into thinking that they were drinking Ribena rather than unadulterated alcohol.

Snakebite   A mixture of lager and cider with an odd cloudy yellow colour; a rite of passage for many teenagers although banned by many pubs because of its highly intoxicating effect.

Construction toys

Meccano   Registered as a trade mark in 1907 by Liverpool clerk Frank Hornby, who had originally called his system Mechanics Made Easy.

Bild-o-brik   Interlocking rubber bricks made from the early 1930s by the Rubber Specialities Company Inc, USA.

Minibrix   Plastic toy construction bricks not unlike Lego, made from the early 1930s by the Premo Rubber Company in Petersfield, Hampshire.

Lego   The firm was established in 1932 in Denmark by master carpenter Ole Kirk Christiansen and began producing "Automatic Binding Bricks" in 1949.

Bayko   Comprised plastic bakelite tiles threaded over thin metal rods, invented by Liverpool entrepreneur Charles Plympton, and sold from 1934.

Bilofix   A bit like wooden Meccano, originally developed by Lego but then split off as a separate company in 1962.

Stickle Bricks   Plastic construction sets for toddlers produced by Denys Fisher from the 1960s.

TV doctors

Ben Casey	US series from 1961-66; starred Vince Edwards and Sam Jaffe; memorable for opening lines: "Man, woman, birth, death, infinity".
Dr Kildare	US series from 1961-66; starred Richard Chamberlain and Raymond Massey; memorable for its theme tune and Richard Chamberlain becoming a heartthrob.
Dr Finlay	British series from 1962-71; starred Bill Simpson, Andrew Cruikshank and Barbara Mullen; memorable for strong Scottish accents.
The Doctors	British series from 1969-71; starred Justine Lord, Nigel Stock and a young Lynda La Plante; memorable for having been written by Fay Weldon (with Elaine Morgan).
The Flying Doctor	Australian series from 1959-60; starred Richard Denning and Jill Adams; memorable for being set in Australia!

Advertising slogans from our youth: clothes and accessories

- Rael-Brook Toplin – the shirt you don't iron.
- The shirt for you is Double Two.
- I pull my Brutus jeans on...
- Put them on your feet, and give your toes a treat (Hush Puppies).
- I dreamed I stopped traffic in my Maidenform bra.
- My girdle is killing me! (Playtex).
- You'll like the way you feel – they'll like the way you look – in your Spirella! (Spirella girdles and bras).
- You care about the shape you're in, So does he, so does he, Wonderful Wonderbra!
- Ticker ticker Timex.
- B – A – double L – I – T - O. Ballito – heavenly nylons.
- Try the new Body Language bra from Playtex, because the bust you always wanted is probably your own.
- If your bra doesn't do all it could for your figure, buy the famous Cross-Your-Heart bra from Playtex, and cross over to a better figure.
- Where's my girdle? Oh, I've got it on! (Silhouette panty girdle).
- Triumph has the bra for the way you are!
- Sarongster's cross-over panels let you move – keep you smooth! (Sarongster girdles).

Spangles flavours

Traditional: Orange, pineapple, blackcurrant, strawberry, lemon and lime.

Old English (according to the advert announcing their launch): Mint humbug (amber); treacle (mustard yellow); liquorice (black); aniseed (green); pear drop (red).

Other varieties of Spangles: acid drop, barley sugar, blackcurrant, liquorice and fizzy orangeade.

National side football managers

England Manager

Walter Winterbottom	1946-62
Alf Ramsey	1963-74
Joe Mercer	1974
Don Revie	1974-77
Ron Greenwood	1977-82
Bobby Robson	1982-90
Graham Taylor	1990-93
Terry Venables	1994-96
Glenn Hoddle	1996-99
Howard Wilkinson	*1999*
Kevin Keegan	1999-2000
Howard Wilkinson	*2000*
Peter Taylor	*2000*
Sven-Göran Eriksson	2001-06
Steve McClaren	2006-08
Fabio Capello	2008-12
Stuart Pearce	*2012*
Roy Hodgson	2012-

Wales Manager

Walley Barnes	1954-55
Jimmy Murphy	1956-64
Dave Bowen	1964-74
Ronnie Burgess	*1965*
Mike Smith	1974-79
Mike England	1979-87
David Williams	*1988*
Terry Yorath	1988-93
John Toshack	1994
Mike Smith	1994-95
Bobby Gould	1995-99
Mark Hughes	1999-2004
John Toshack	2004-10
Brian Flynn	*2010*
Gary Speed	2010-2011
Chris Coleman	2012-

Italics = Caretaker manager

Scotland Manager

Andy Beattie	1954
Dawson Walker	1958
Matt Busby	1958
Andy Beattie	1959-60
Ian McColl	1960-65
Jock Stein	1965-66
John Prentice	1966
Malcolm MacDonald	1966-67
Bobby Brown	1967-71
Tommy Docherty	1971-72
Willie Ormond	1973-77
Ally MacLeod	1977-78
Jock Stein	1978-85
Alex Ferguson	1985-86
Andy Roxburgh	1986-93
Craig Brown	1993-02
Berti Vogts	2002-04
Tommy Burns	2004
Walter Smith	2004-07
Alex McLeish	2007
George Burley	2008-09
Craig Levein	2009-2012
Billy Stark	*2012*
Gordon Strachan	2012-

Northern Ireland Manager

Peter Doherty	1951-62
Bertie Peacock	1962-67
Billy Bingham	1967-71
Terry Neill	1971-75
Dave Clements	1975-76
Danny Blanchflower	1976-79
Billy Bingham	1980-94
Bryan Hamilton	1994-98
Lawrie McMenemy	1998-99
Sammy McIlroy	2000-03
Lawrie Sanchez	2004-07
Nigel Worthington	2007-2011
Michael O'Neill	2012-

Advertising slogans from our youth: alcohol

- Don't be vague, ask for Haig (whiskey).
- Coates comes up from Somerset, where the cider apples grow.
- Double Diamond – the beer the men drink.
- A Double Diamond works wonders, works wonders, a Double Diamond works wonders so drink one today!
- Always pick Flowers!
- Harp – stays sharp to the bottom of the glass.
- Heinken – refreshes the parts other beers cannot reach.
- I'd love a Babycham.
- Carlsberg – probably the best lager in the world.
- Courage – it's what your right arm's for.
- Do 'ave a Dubonnet.
- Smile, please – you're in Greenall Whitley land!
- My Goodness, My Guinness.
- What we want is Watney's.
- What about a Worthington?

Confectionery manufacturer mergers

Company	Taken over by/ merged with	Year of take over/merger
Fry's	Cadbury's	1919
Wilkinson's	Bassett's	1961
Barrett's	Bassett's	1966
Mackintosh's	Rowntree	1969
Rowntree Mackintosh	Nestlé	1988
Trebor	Cadbury's	1989
Bassett's	Cadbury's	1989
Terry's	Kraft	1993
Cadbury's	Kraft	2010

British film certification

1932- 51 **U** (For "Universal" – Suitable for everyone including children).
A (For "Adult" – Some councils ruled that children
must be accompanied by an adult).
H (For "Horror" – Some councils ruled that only those over 16
could be admitted).

1951-70 **U** (As before).
A (As before).
X (Suitable for those aged 16 and over and enforced by all councils).

1970- 82 **U** (As before).
A (Children aged over 5 admitted, although parents were advised
they might not want children under 14 to see the film).
AA (Suitable only for those aged 14 and older).
X (Suitable only for those aged 18 and older).

Cinema ticket prices from the past

When cinemas were vast places with hundreds of seats and just one screen,
you had a choice between front stalls, rear stalls, front circle and rear circle
with varying ticket prices, but the average prices were as follows:

Year	Ticket price	Today's equivalent
1940	10d	4p
1945	1s 5d	7p
1950	1s 6d	7.5p
1955	1s 9d	9p
1960	2s 6d	12.5p
1965	3s 9d	19p
1970	6s	30p

Who was in which *Carry On* film?

	Released	KW	CH	JS	SJ	KC	HJ	BB	PB	BW	JD	JDo	LP
Carry On Sergeant	1958	*	*			*	*						
Carry On Nurse	1959	*	*	*		*	*						*
Carry On Teacher	1959	*	*	*		*	*						*
Carry On Constable	1960	*	*	*	*	*	*						*
Carry On Regardless	1961	*	*	*	*	*	*						
Carry On Cruising	1962	*			*	*							
Carry On Cabby	1963		*		*	*	*					*	
Carry On Jack	1963	*	*										
Carry On Spying	1964	*	*							*	*		
Carry On Cleo	1964	*	*	*	*	*					*		
Carry On Cowboy	1965	*	*	*	*				*	*	*		
Carry On Screaming	1966	*	*	*					*	*	*		
Don't Lose Your Head	1966	*	*	*	*						*		
Follow That Camel	1967	*	*	*					*	*	*		
Carry On Doctor	1967	*	*	*	*	*		*	*	*	*		
Carry On Up the Khyber	1968	*	*	*	*				*	*			
Carry On Camping	1969	*	*	*	*			*	*	*			
Carry On Again Doctor	1969	*	*	*	*	*			*	*	*		
Carry On Up the Jungle	1970		*	*	*	*		*					
Carry On Loving	1970	*	*	*	*			*	*	*			
Carry On Henry	1971	*	*	*	*	*			*	*			
Carry On At Your Convenience	1971	*	*	*	*			*	*				
Carry On Matron	1972	*	*	*	*	*	*	*		*		*	
Carry On Abroad	1972	*	*	*	*	*	*	*		*		*	
Carry On Girls	1973			*	*	*		*	*	*		*	
Carry On Dick	1974	*		*	*	*	*	*	*	*		*	
Carry On Behind	1975	*		*		*		*	*			*	
Carry On England	1976		*			*			*			*	
Total appearances		24	23	23	19	16	14	14	13	9	9	6	3

Key

KW	Kenneth Williams	BB	Bernard Bresslaw
CH	Charles Hawtrey	PB	Peter Butterworth
JS	Joan Sims	BW	Barbara Windsor
SJ	Sid James	JD	Jim Dale
KC	Kenneth Connor	JDo	Jack Douglas
HJ	Hattie Jacques	LP	Leslie Phillips

Roman roads

Ermine Street:	From Bishopsgate in London (Londinium) to Lincoln (Lindum Colonia) and eventually York (Eboracum).
Watling Street:	From Dover (Portus Dubris) through Canterbury (Durovernum), London, St Albans (Verulamium), Lichfield (Letocetum) and on to Wroxeter (Viroconium).
Via Devana:	From Colchester (Colonia Victricensis) through Cambridge (Durolipons), Godmanchester (Durovigutum), Corby, Mancetter (Manduessedum), along Watling Street to Water Eaton (Pennocrucium), then Newport, Shropshire (Plesc) to Whitchurch (Mediolanum) and Chester (Deva).
The Fosse Way:	From Exeter (Isca Dumnoniorum) through Ilchester (Lindinis), Bath (Aquae Sulis), Cirencester (Corinium) and Leicester (Ratae Corieltauvorum) to Lincoln (Lindum Colonia).

Other Roman place names

Aquae Sulis	Bath	Glevum Colonia	Gloucester
Aquae Arnemetiae	Buxton	Hortonium	Halifax
Luguvalium	Carlisle	Vectis	Isle of Wight
Caesaromagus	Chelmsford	Mamucium	Manchester
Vindolanda	Chesterholme	Pons Aelius	Newcastle upon Tyne
Concangis	Chester-le-Street	Oxonium, Oxonia	Oxford
Noviomagus	Chichester	Durolitum	Romford
Danum	Doncaster	Calleva Atrebatum	Silchester
Durnovaria	Dorchester	Durocornovium	Swindon
Dubris	Dover	Calcaria	Tadcaster
Durocobrivis	Dunstable	Lactodorum	Towcester
Dunelmum	Durham	Venta Belgarum	Winchester
Sulloniacis	Edgware		

Ads from US import comics

Sea Monkeys
Own a Bowlfull of Happiness – Instant Pets! Only $1.25

Charles Atlas
The Insult That Made a Man Out of Mac!
Let me prove I can make you a new man!
Mail coupon now for my 32-page illustrated book.

Exciting Ant Farm
An Ant's Entire World! Complete With Stock of Live Ants! Only $2.98

Scary Life-Size Monster Ghost!
Obeys Your Commands! Over 7 feet tall! Only $1.00.

Treasure Chest of Fun:
X-Ray Specs (see bones thru skin!) $1.00.

Joy Buzzer (the most popular joke novelty in years!
When you shake hands it almost raises the victim off his feet) only 50c.

Secret Spy Scope (handy for sporting events,
counter-spying and girl watching) $2.98.

Trick black soap (victim washes face and gets blacker and blacker) only 25c.

See Behind Glasses (really comes in handy at times) 75c.

Surprise package (are you willing to take a chance?
We won't tell you what you get, but because you're willing to gamble,
we'll give you more than your money's worth) only 50c.

Throw Your Voice (…into trunks, behind doors, everywhere) only 25c.

Onion Gum (looks like real chewing gum… it's too funny!) 20c.

Worms (drop these seemingly innocent pellets into a glass of water
and magically a worm will appear) 15c.

Whoopee cushion (watch the fun when someone sits down!
It gives forth embarrassing noises) 50c.

Picture card series issued in packs of PG Tips tea

Catalogue number	Title	Year of issue
B1	British Birds	1954
B2	Wild Flowers Series 1	1955
B3	Out into Space	1956
B4	Bird Portraits	1957
B5	British Wild Life	1958
B6	Wild Flowers Series 2	1959
B7	Freshwater Fish	1960
B8	African Wild Life	1961
B9	Tropical Birds	1961
B10	Asian Wild Life	1962
B11	British Butterflies	1963
B12	Wildlife in Danger	1963
B13	Wild Flowers Series 3	1964
B14	Butterflies of the World	1964
B15	Wild Birds in Britain	1965
B16	Transport Through the Ages	1966
B17	Trees in Britain	1966
B18	Flags and Emblems of the World	1967
B19	British Costumes	1968
B20	History of the Motor Car	1968
B21	Famous People	1969
B22	The Saga of Ships	1970
B23	The Race into Space	1971
B24	Prehistoric Animals	1971
B25	History of Aviation	1972
B26	Adventurers and Explorers	1973
B27	The Sea – Our Other World	1974
B28	Inventors and Inventions	1975
B29	Wonders of Wildlife	1975
B30	Play Better Soccer	1976
B31	Police File	1977
B32	Vanishing Wildlife	1978
B33	Olympic Greats	1979
B34	Woodland Wildlife	1980

Years TV series began:
entertainment, quiz and game shows

1950	*Come Dancing*
1951	*What's My Line?*
1955	*Sunday Night at the London Palladium; Take Your Pick; Double Your Money*
1956	*The $64,000 Question; Opportunity Knocks*
1958	*Songs of Praise; The White Heather Club*
1961	*Points of View*
1962	*Top of the Form; University Challenge*
1965	*Call My Bluff*
1966	*It's a Knockout*
1967	*Ask the Family; The Golden Shot*
1971	*The Generation Game; The Sky's the Limit*
1972	*Mastermind; Sale of the Century*
1973	*New Faces*
1974	*The Wheeltappers and Shunters Social Club*
1978	*3-2-1*
1979	*Give Us a Clue*

"Underground" magazines
from the 1960s and '70s

Black Dwarf:	started 1968.
Friends/Frendz:	started in 1969.
Gandalf's Garden:	started in 1968.
Ink:	started in 1971.
International Times (IT):	started 1966.
Oz:	started in UK in 1967.

Latin first conjugation active verbs

Latin verb tenses:

Present, eg. I carry, I am carrying   Perfect, eg. I carried
Imperfect, eg. I was carrying   Future, eg. I will carry
Pluperfect, eg. I had carried   Future imperfect, eg. I will have carried

| | *Present active indicative* | | *Perfect active indicative* | |
	Singular	**Plural**	**Singular**	**Plural**
First person	porto	portamus	portavi	portavimus
Second person	portas	portatis	portavisti	portavistis
Third person	portat	portant	portavit	portaverunt

| | *Imperfect active indicative* | | *Future active indicative* | |
	Singular	**Plural**	**Singular**	**Plural**
First person	portabam	portabamus	portabo	portabimus
Second person	portabas	portabatis	portabis	portabitis
Third person	portabat	portabant	portabit	portabunt

| | *Pluperfect active indicative* | | *Future perfect active indicative* | |
	Singular	**Plural**	**Singular**	**Plural**
First person	portaveram	portaveramus	portavero	portaverimus
Second person	portaveras	portaveratis	portaveris	portaveritis
Third person	portaverat	portaverant	portaverit	portaverint

1950s school dinner staples

Spam fritters • Mince. • Sausages • Meat pie *(with gristle in it)*
Fish *(on Fridays)* • Macaroni cheese • Mashed potato *(with lumps)*
Watery boiled potatoes • "Greens" • Carrots • Peas
Semolina pudding *(with a splodge of red jam)* • Rice pudding
Tapioca pudding • Fruit pie with custard

Soap operas of the past

Mrs Dale's Diary

BBC radio series, 1948 to 1969; concerned doctor's wife Mrs Mary Dale, her husband Jim, her sister Sally (whose husband turned out to be gay), daughter Gwen, son Bob, his wife Jenny and their twins and Mrs Dale's mother, Mrs Freeman. Mrs Dale was played by Ellis Peters until she was controversially replaced by Jessie Matthews in 1963.

The Appleyards

A BBC TV soap opera for children about the Appleyard family, living in the Home Counties. Broadcast between 1952 and 1957.

Emergency Ward Ten

ITV hospital drama, set in Oxbridge General, which ran from 1957 to 1967; featured Jill Browne as Nurse Carole Young, Charles "Bud" Tingwell (Dr. Alan Dawson), Desmond Carrington (Dr. Chris Anderson).

Compact

BBC drama, 1962 to 1965 concerning the world of magazine publishing; starred Jean Harvey as editor Joanne Minster and later Ronald Allen as Ian Harmon.

Crossroads

Legendary ITV soap opera which ran from 1964; set at the Crossroads Motel near Birmingham. Starred Noele Gordon as Meg Richardson, Roger Tonge (son Sandy), Jane Rossington (daughter Jill), Beryl Johnstone (sister Kitty) and not forgetting Ann George (Amy Turtle) and Paul Henry (Benny Hawkins).

The Newcomers

BBC series, 1965 to 1969; centred on the Cooper family who moved from London to the fictional country town of Angleton; starred Alan Browning as the father, Ellis Cooper, Maggie Fitzgibbon as his wife Vivienne and Judy Geeson as daughter Maria.

Waggoner's Walk

BBC Radio 2's replacement for Mrs Dale, but with a much harder edge. Set in Hampstead, it was broadcast from 1969 to 1980 and began with its roots firmly in the Swinging Sixties, and embraced topical themes including abortion, homosexuality, murder and student protest. Mike and Claire Nash (Edward Cast and Ellen McIntosh), the owners of Number 1 Waggoner's Walk, were a constant presence in a cast subject to frequent changes.

Catchphrases from the golden age of TV

"Falob-a-dob!"	Bill and Ben	*The Flowerpot Men*
"Wee-ed!"	Little Weed	*The Flowerpot Men*
"Was it Bill or was it Ben?"	The narrator	*The Flowerpot Men*
"I'm in charge!"	Bruce Forsyth	*Sunday Night At London Palladium*
"Take the money!" "Open the box!"	The audience	*Take Your Pick*
"You dirty old man!"	Harold Steptoe	*Steptoe And Son*
"Silly moo!"	Alf Garnett	*Till Death Us Do Part*
"It stands to reason!"	Alf Garnett	*Till Death Us Do Part*
"Just like that!"	Tommy Cooper	
"You stupid boy!"	Captain Mainwaring	*Dad's Army*
"Don't panic!"	Corporal Jones	*Dad's Army*
"They don't like it up 'em!"	Corporal Jones	*Dad's Army*
"We're all doomed!"	Private Frazer	*Dad's Army*
"Here's one I made earlier."	Valerie Singleton	*Blue Peter*)
"Can you guess what it is yet?"	Rolf Harris	
"I've started so I'll finish."	Magnus Magnusson	*Mastermind*
"Oo! You are awful – but I like you!"	Mandy	*The Dick Emery Show*
"Get out of that!"	Morecambe and Wise	
"What do you think of it so far?" "Ruggish!"	Morecambe and Wise	
"You can't see the join!"	Morecambe and Wise	
"Good night, and may your God go with you."	Dave Allen	
"And it's goodnight from me." "And it's goodnight from him"	The Two Ronnies	
"I'm free!"	Mr Humphries	*Are You Being Served?*
"Que?"	Manuel	*Fawlty Towers*

UK Entries in the Eurovision Song Contest

Year	Song	Artist	Position
1957	"All"	Patricia Bredin	7
1959	"Sing Little Birdie"	Teddy Johnson and Pearl Carr	2
1960	"Looking High, High, High"	Bryan Johnson	2
1961	"Are You Sure"	The Allisons	2
1962	"Ring a Ding Girl"	Ronnie Carroll	4
1963	"Say Wonderful Things"	Ronnie Carroll	4
1964	"I Love the Little Things"	Matt Monro	2
1965	"I Belong"	Kathy Kirby	2
1966	"A Man Without Love"	Kenneth McKellar	9
1967	"Puppet on a String"	Sandie Shaw	1
1968	"Congratulations"	Cliff Richard	2
1969	"Boom Bang-A-Bang"	Lulu	1*
1970	"Knock, Knock, Who's There"	Mary Hopkin	2
1971	"Jack in the Box"	Clodagh Rodgers	4
1972	"Beg, Steal or Borrow"	The New Seekers	2
1973	"Power to All Our Friends"	Cliff Richard	3
1974	"Long Live Love"	Olivia Newton-John	4
1975	"Let Me Be the One"	The Shadows	2
1976	"Save Your Kisses For Me"	Brotherhood Of Man	1
1977	"Rock Bottom"	Lynsey de Paul and Mike Moran	2
1978	"The Bad Old Days"	Co-Co	11
1979	"Mary Ann"	Black Lace	7
1980	"Love Enough For Two"	Prima Donna	3
1981	"Making Your Mind Up"	Bucks Fizz	1

* *Joint winner with three other entries!*

There were no UK entries in 1956 or 1958.

Hanna-Barbera TV cartoon series

Cartoon	First produced	Main characters
The Huckleberry Hound Show	1958	Huckleberry Hound.
Yogi Bear	1958	Yogi Bear, Boo Boo and Ranger Smith.
Pixie and Dixie and Mr. Jinks	1958	Mr Jinks the cat, and Pixie and Dixie the mice.
The Flintstones	1960	Fred and Wilma Flintstone, their daughter Pebbles, their dinosaur Dino, Barney and Betty Rubble and their son Bamm Bamm.
Top Cat	1961	Top Cat, Benny the Ball, Choo Choo, Fancy Fancy, Spook, Brain, Officer Dibble.
The Jetsons	1962	George and Jane Jetson, their children Judy and Elroy, their dog Astro and their robot maid Rosie.
The Magilla Gorilla Show	1964	Magilla Gorilla and pet shop owner Mr Peebles.
Squiddly Diddly	1965	Squiddly Diddly the octopus, Chief Winchley.
Frankenstein, Jr. and the Impossibles	1966	Frankenstein Jr, Buzz Conroy and his dad Professor Conroy, Multi Man, Fluid Man and Coil Man.
The Banana Splits Adventure Hour	1968	Fleegle, Bingo, Drooper and Snork.
Wacky Races	1968	Dick Dastardly and Muttley, Penelope Pitstop, Peter Perfect, The Ant Hill Mob, the Slag Brothers, the Gruesome Twosome, Professor Pat Pending, Red Max, Sergeant Blast and Private Meekley, Luke and Blubber Bear, Rufus Ruffcut and Sawtooth.
The Perils of Penelope Pitstop	1969	Penelope Pitstop, the Hooded Claw and the Ant Hill Mob.
Dastardly and Muttley in Their Flying Machines	1969	Dick Dastardly, Muttley, Zilly, Klunk and Yankee Doodle Pigeon.
It's the Wolf	1969	Mildew Wolf, Lambsy and Bristle Hound the dog.
Scooby-Doo, Where Are You!	1969	Freddie, Daphne, Velma, Shaggy and Scooby-Doo.
Harlem Globetrotters	1970	Meadowlark Lemon, Curly Neal, Geese Ausbie, Gip, Bobby Joe Mason, Pablo Robertson, their bus driver and manager Granny and their dog Dribbles.
Josie and the Pussycats	1970	Josie McCoy, tambourinist Valerie, drummer Melody, their manager Alexander Cabot III, his sister Alexandra, her cat Sebastian and their roadie Alan.
Help!... It's the Hair Bear Bunch!	1971	Hair Bear, Bubi Bear, Square Bear, the zoo director Mr. Eustace P. Peevly and his assistant Lionel J Botch.
The Funky Phantom	1971	Skip, April and their dog Augie and the Funky Phantom, Jonathan Wellington. "Mudsy" Muddlemore and his cat Boo.
Wait Till Your Father Gets Home	1972	Harry and Irma Boyle, their children Alice, Chet and Jamie and their next-door neighbour Ralph.
Inch High, Private Eye	1973	Inch High, his neice Lori, her friend Gator, their dog Braveheart and his boss Mr Finkerton.
Hong Kong Phooey	1974	Penrod Penry Pooch, aka Hong Kong Phooey, Sergeant Flint, Rosemary the telephone operator.

Green Shield Stamps

Green Shield Stamps were an early form of loyalty scheme. They were issued to customers by shops such as independent grocers, fishmongers and butchers who proudly displayed signs saying "We give Green Shield Stamps". Later even Tesco started giving the stamps.

Green Shield Stamps were introduced by London businessman Richard Tompkins who had seen S&H Green Stamps in the USA. When S&H launched in the UK they were known as Pink Stamps and were issued by the supermarket chain Fine Fare. The Co-op also began issuing Dividend Stamps.

Shoppers were given one Green Shield stamp for every 6d they spent and needed 1,280 stamps in order to fill one Green Shield Stamps book. If you saved up enough books, you could exchange them for goods such as these listed in the 1965 catalogue:

> Regentone 19in television (88 books).
> Longines 9ct Gold watch (39½ books).
> Kenwood Chef (33¼ books).
> Kodak Brownie 8 movie camera (13¼ books).
> Silver Cloud motor boat (170 books !?!).

Or for just one book you could get any one of the following items:

> A set of six mugs in pastel colours;
> A record rack;
> A mouth organ;
> A gent's brush and comb set;
> A set of stainless steel salad servers;
> A set of three pictures.

In the 1970s, enthusiasm for Green Shield Stamps began to decline, forcing Tompkins to adapt the concept of his catalogue shops. Instead of paying for goods chosen from the catalogue with stamps, customers could pay with money! So if you are wondering what happened to the old Green Shield Stamps shops, look no further than your local branch of Argos!

Wimbledon champions

Year	Men's Singles	Ladies' Singles
1950	Budge Patty (USA)	Louise Brough (USA)
1951	Dick Savitt (USA)	Doris Hart (USA)
1952	Frank Sedgman (Australia)	Maureen Connolly (USA)
1953	Vic Seixas (USA)	Maureen Connolly (USA)
1954	Jaroslav Drobny (Egypt)	Maureen Connolly (USA)
1955	Tony Trabert (USA)	Louise Brough (USA)
1956	Lew Hoad (Australia)	Shirley Fry Irvin (USA)
1957	Lew Hoad (Australia)	Althea Gibson (USA)
1958	Ashley Cooper (Australia)	Althea Gibson (USA)
1959	Alex Olmedo (USA)	Maria Bueno (Brazil)
1960	Neale Fraser (Australia)	Maria Bueno (Brazil)
1961	Rod Laver (Australia)	Angela Mortimer (GB)
1962	Rod Laver (Australia)	Karen Hantze Susman (USA)
1963	Chuck McKinley (USA)	Margaret Court (Australia)
1964	Roy Emerson (Australia)	Maria Bueno (Brazil)
1965	Roy Emerson (Australia)	Margaret Court (Australia)
1966	Manuel Santana (Spain)	Billie Jean King (USA)
1967	John Newcombe (Australia)	Billie Jean King (USA)
1968	Rod Laver (Australia)	Billie Jean King (USA)
1969	Rod Laver (Australia)	Ann Haydon-Jones (GB)
1970	John Newcombe (Australia)	Margaret Court (Australia)
1971	John Newcombe (Australia)	Evonne Goolagong (Australia)
1972	Stan Smith (USA)	Billie Jean King (USA)
1973	Jan Kodeš (Czechoslovakia)	Billie Jean King (USA)
1974	Jimmy Connors (USA)	Chris Evert (USA)
1975	Arthur Ashe (USA)	Billie Jean King (USA)
1976	Björn Borg (Sweden)	Chris Evert (USA)
1977	Björn Borg (Sweden)	Virginia Wade (GB)
1978	Björn Borg (Sweden)	Martina Navrátilová (USA)
1979	Björn Borg (Sweden)	Martina Navrátilová (USA)
1980	Björn Borg (Sweden)	Evonne Goolagong Cawley (Australia)
1981	John McEnroe (USA)	Chris Evert (USA)

British bank note illustrations

	Illustration	Date issued	Withdrawn
£1	Sir Isaac Newton with book, telescope and prism	February 9, 1978	March 11, 1988
£5	Duke of Wellington / battle scene	November 11, 1971	November 29, 1991
£5	George Stephenson / the "Rocket"	June 7, 1990	November 21, 2003
£5	Elizabeth Fry / reading to inmates in Newgate prison	May 21, 2002	
£10	Florence Nightingale / army hospital at Scutari during the Crimean War	February 20, 1975	May 20, 1994
£10	Charles Dickens / scene from the Pickwick Papers	April 29, 1992	July 31, 2003
£10	Charles Darwin/ HMS *Beagle* / hummingbird, flowers and magnifying glass	November 7, 2000	
£20	William Shakespeare / *Romeo and Juliet* balcony scene	July 9, 1970	March 19, 1993
£20	Michael Faraday / Royal Institution Lectures	June 5, 1991	February 28, 2001
£20	Sir Edward Elgar / Worcester Cathedral	June 22, 1999	July 1, 2010
£20	Adam Smith/ pin factory	March 13, 2007	
£50	Sir Christopher Wren / plan of St Paul's Cathedral	March 20, 1981	September 20, 1996
£50	Sir John Houblon	April 20, 1994	
£50	James Watt and Matthew Boulton	November 2, 2011	

Highest-rated TV shows between 1950 and 1989

Programme	Additional information	Broadcast	Audience (in millions)
The World Cup final 1966	England 4 West Germany 2 at Wembley.	July 30, 1966	32.3
The Royal Family	Documentary about life with the royals.	June 21, 1969 (BBC1), June 28, 1969 (ITV)	30.69
EastEnders	When Den presented Angie with divorce papers.	December 25, 1986	30.15
Apollo 13 splashdown	End of the near-disastrous mission.	April 17, 1970	28.6
FA Cup Final replay	Chelsea 2 Leeds 1 at Old Trafford.	April 29, 1970	28.49
Royal Wedding ceremony	The wedding of Charles and Diana.	July 29, 1981	28.4
Princess Anne's Wedding	Princess Anne married Captain Mark Phillips.	November 14, 1973	27.6
Coronation Street	Alan Bradley was killed by a Blackpool tram.	December 8, 1989	26.93
Royal Variety Performance 1965	Featured Shirley Bassey, and Peter Cook and Dudley Moore.	November 14, 1965	24.2
News	John F. Kennedy's assassination	November 22, 1963	24.15
To the Manor Born	Final episode of the first series.	November 11, 1979	23.95
Miss World		November 20, 1970	23.76
Miss World		November 19, 1967	23.76
The Royal Variety Performance 1975	Featured among others Bruce Forsyth, the cast of *Dad's Army*, Count Basie, Harry Secombe, Vera Lynn, Telly Savalas and Charles Aznavour.	November 16, 1975	22.66
Apollo 8 splashdown		December 27, 1968	22.55

Programme	Additional information	Broadcast	Audience (in millions)
This Is Your Life	The first episode to feature a member of the royal family, Lord Mountbatten.	April 27, 1977	22.22
Sunday Night at the London Palladium	The final episode of the long-running variety show.	December 3, 1967	21.89
The Benny Hill Show		March 24, 1971	21.67
Dallas	Kristin Shepard was revealed to have shot J R.	November 22, 1980	21.6
Eurovision Song Contest 1973	Cliff Richard represented the UK. with "Power To All Our Friends". The winner was the Finnish entry "Tom Tom Tom" by Marion Rung.	April 7, 1973	21.56
To the Manor Born	The final episode of series 2.	November 11, 1980	21.55
Steptoe and Son	The final episode of series 3.	February 18, 1964	21.54
The Mike Yarwood Christmas Show	Broadcast just before the more often remembered 1977 Morecambe and Wise Christmas Show	December 25, 1977	21.4
Coronation Street	Annie Walker had disappeared. The episode also featured Rita's only appearance until she was brought back as a regular character in 1972.	December 2, 1964	21.36
The Morecambe and Wise Show	Guests included Elton John, the stars of The Good Life, James Hunt, Angela Rippon (returning after her legendary dance routine the previous Christmas), Michael Parkinson and various other BBC presenters performing 'There Is Nothing Like A Dame'. It was also Eric and Ernie's last BBC show.	December 25, 1977	21.3
Sale of the Century		December 24, 1978	21.15
Boxing: Ali vs. Frazier	"The Fight of the Century" from Madison Square Garden. Joe Frazier won after 15 rounds.	March 9, 1971	21.12

Decimalization

Britain introduced decimal currency on "D-Day" – Monday, February 15, 1971.

Introductory packs were issued presenting the new ½p, 1p, 2p, 5p and 10p coins and the country was advised what their old pennies would be worth in the new decimal currency.

Old pence	New pence (what we were told it was worth)	New pence (what it was actually worth)
1d	½ p	0.4p
2d	1p*	0.8p
3d	1p*	1.3p
4d	1 ½ p	1.7p
5d	2p	2.1p
6d	2 ½ p	2.5p
7d	3p	2.9p
8d	3 ½ p	3.3p
9d	4p*	3.8p
10d	4p*	4.2p
11d	4 ½ p	4.6p
1s	5p	5p

Yes, people were taught and seemed to accept that different values of old pence were now equivalent to identical values of new pence!

Doctor Who's top 10 most persistent enemies

1. The Daleks.

2. The Cybermen.

3. The Master.

4. The Sontarans.

5. The Silurians.

6. The Ice Warriors.

7. Davros.

8. The Black Guardian.

9. The Autons.

10. Borusa.

TV cops and Detectives

Name	Series	Started	Sidekick	Trademark
Sexton Blake (Laurence Payne)	*Sexton Blake*	1967 (ITV)	Tinker (Roger Foss)	Pipe
Jules Maigret (Rupert Davies)	*Maigret*	1960 (BBC)	Lucas (Ewen Solon)	Pipe
George Dixon (Jack Warner)	*Dixon of Dock Green*	1955 (BBC)	Andy Crawford (Peter Byrne)	"Evening all" under blue lamp
Frank Columbo (Peter Falk)	*Columbo*	1968 (BBC)	"Dog"	Shabby raincoat
Frank Marker (Alfred Burke)	*Public Eye*	1965 (ITV)	Nobody	"Six guineas a day plus expenses"
Theo Kojak (Telly Savalas)	*Kojak*	1973 (BBC)	Bobby Crocker (Kevin Dobson)	Bald head and lollipop
Frank Cannon (William Conrad)	*Cannon*	1971	Bobby Kester (Blaine H. McKee)	Overweight and balding
Sam McCloud (Dennis Weaver)	*McCloud*	1970	Joe Broadhurst (Terry Carter)	Cowboy hat
Charlie Barlow (Stratford Johns)	*Z Cars and Softly Softly*	1962 and 1966 (BBC)	John Watt (Frank Windsor)	Overweight (later in series titled *Barlow At Large*)
Tom Lockhart (Raymond Francis)	*No Hiding Place*	1959 (ITV)	Harry Baxter (Eric Lander)	Homburg hat and moustache
Robert Fabian (Bruce Seton)	*Fabian of the Yard*	1954 (BBC)	DS Wyatt (Robert Raglan)	Pipe

Other confectionery manufacturers

Nestlé   Formed in 1905 by the merger of the Anglo-Swiss Milk Company and Farine Lactée Henri Nestlé. The Milky Bar launched in 1937. The Milky Bar Kid first appeared in TV adverts in 1961.

Bassett's   George Bassett and Co Ltd was founded in Sheffield in 1842. They began manufacturing Liquorice Allsorts around 1900, while Jelly Babies were launched in 1918 as Peace Babies to celebrate the end of World War One.

Trebor   Trebor was founded in 1907 as Robertson and Woodcock. They became Trebor (founder Robert Robertson's name backwards). Trebor Mints were launched in 1935, Trebor Extra Strong Mints in 1937 and Murray Mints in 1944.

Matlows   Matlow Bros was formed in London by Alf and Maurice Matlow. They formed Swizzels Ltd in 1933 and began production of Love Hearts.

Duncan's   Duncan's of Edinburgh were the original creators of the Walnut Whip, which they first sold in 1910. The original Walnut Whip contained two walnuts, one on the top and on inside the shell.

Fry's   Joseph Fry had begun making chocolate in 1759. The Fry's Chocolate Cream bar dates from 1866 and Fry's Turkish Delight from 1914. Fry's also sold Britain's first chocolate Easter eggs in 1873. The Fry's name continued to be used although the company merged with Cadbury's in 1919.

"Pirate" and offshore radio stations of the 1960s

Radio Veronica:	started 1960.
Radio Caroline:	started 1964.
Radio London:	started 1964.
Swinging Radio England:	started 1966.
Radio Jackie:	started 1969.

American Academy Award winners 1945-80

	Best film	Best director
1945	*The Lost Weekend*	Billy Wilder (*The Lost Weekend*)
1946	*The Best Years of Our Lives*	William Wyler (*The Best Years of Our Lives*)
1947	*Gentleman's Agreement*	Elia Kazan (*Gentleman's Agreement*)
1948	*Hamlet*	John Huston (*The Treasure of the Sierra Madre*)
1949	*All the King's Men*	Joseph L. Mankiewicz (*A Letter to Three Wives*)
1950	*All About Eve*	Joseph L. Mankiewicz (*All About Eve*)
1951	*An American in Paris*	George Stevens (*A Place in the Sun*)
1952	*The Greatest Show on Earth*	John Ford (*The Quiet Man*)
1953	*From Here to Eternity*	Fred Zinnemann (*From Here to Eternity*)
1954	*On the Waterfront*	Elia Kazan (*On the Waterfront*)
1955	*Marty*	Delbert Mann (*Marty*)
1956	*Around the World in Eighty Days*	George Stevens (*Giant*)
1957	*The Bridge on the River Kwai*	David Lean (*The Bridge on the River Kwai*)
1958	*Gigi*	Vincente Minnelli (*Gigi*)
1959	*Ben-Hur*	William Wyler (*Ben-Hur*)
1960	*The Apartment*	Billy Wilder (*The Apartment*)
1961	*West Side Story*	Robert Wise and Jerome Robbins (*West Side Story*)
1962	*Lawrence of Arabia*	David Lean (*Lawrence of Arabia*)
1963	*Tom Jones*	Tony Richardson (*Tom Jones*)
1964	*My Fair Lady*	George Cukor (*My Fair Lady*)
1965	*The Sound of Music*	Robert Wise (*The Sound of Music*)
1966	*A Man For All Seasons*	Fred Zinnemann (*A Man For All Seasons*)
1967	*In the Heat of the Night*	Mike Nichols (*The Graduate*)
1968	*Oliver!*	Carol Reed (*Oliver!*)
1969	*Midnight Cowboy*	John Schlesinger (*Midnight Cowboy*)
1970	*Patton*	Franklin J. Schaffner (*Patton*)
1971	*The French Connection*	William Friedkin (*The French Connection*)
1972	*The Godfather*	Bob Fosse (*Cabaret*)
1973	*The Sting*	George Roy Hill (*The Sting*)
1974	*The Godfather Part II*	Francis Ford Coppola (*The Godfather Part II*)
1975	*One Flew Over the Cuckoo's Nest*	Milos Forman (*One Flew Over the Cuckoo's Nest*)
1976	*Rocky*	John G. Avildsen (*Rocky*)
1977	*Annie Hall*	Woody Allen (*Annie Hall*)
1978	*The Deer Hunter*	Michael Cimino (*The Deer Hunter*)
1979	*Kramer vs. Kramer*	Robert Benton (*Kramer vs. Kramer*)
1980	*Ordinary People*	Robert Redford (*Ordinary People*)

American Academy Award winners 1945-62

	Best Actor	Best Actress
1945	Ray Milland (*The Lost Weekend*)	Joan Crawford (*Mildred Pierce*)
1946	Fredric March (*The Best Years of our Lives*)	Olivia de Havilland (*To Each His Own*)
1947	Ronald Colman (*A Double Life*)	Loretta Young (*The Farmer's Daughter*)
1948	Laurence Olivier (*Hamlet*)	Jane Wyman (*Johnny Belinda*)
1949	Broderick Crawford (*All The King's Men*)	Olivia de Havilland (*The Heiress*)
1950	José Ferrer (*Cyrano de Bergerac*)	Judy Holliday (*Born Yesterday*)
1951	Humphrey Bogart (*The African Queen*)	Vivien Leigh (*A Streetcar Named Desire*)
1952	Gary Cooper (*High Noon*)	Shirley Booth (*Come Back, Little Sheba*)
1953	William Holden (*Stalag 17*)	Audrey Hepburn (*Roman Holiday*)
1954	Marlon Brando (*On the Waterfront*)	Grace Kelly (*The Country Girl*)
1955	Ernest Borgnine (*Marty*)	Anna Magnani (*The Rose Tattoo*)
1956	Yul Brynner (*The King and I*)	Ingrid Bergman (*Anastasia*)
1957	Alec Guinness (*The Bridge on the River Kwai*)	Joanne Woodward (*The Three Faces of Eve*)
1958	David Niven (*Separate Tables*)	Susan Hayward (*I Want to Live!*)
1959	Charlton Heston (*Ben-Hur*)	Simone Signoret (*Room at the Top*)
1960	Burt Lancaster (*Elmer Gantry*)	Elizabeth Taylor (*Butterfield 8*)
1961	Maximilian Schell (*Judgment at Nuremberg*)	Sophia Loren (*Two Women*)
1962	Gregory Peck (*To Kill a Mockingbird*)	Anne Bancroft (*The Miracle Worker*)

American Academy Award winners 1963-80

	Best Actor	Best Actress
1963	Sidney Poitier *(Lilies of The Field)*	Patricia Neal *(Hud)*
1964	Rex Harrison *(My Fair Lady)*	Julie Andrews *(Mary Poppins)*
1965	Lee Marvin *(Cat Ballou)*	Julie Christie *(Darling)*
1966	Paul Scofield *(A Man For All Seasons)*	Elizabeth Taylor *(Who's Afraid of Virginia Woolf?)*
1967	Rod Steiger *(In the Heat of the Night)*	Katharine Hepburn *(Guess Who's Coming to Dinner)*
1968	Cliff Robertson *(Charly)*	*(tie):* Katharine Hepburn *(The Lion in Winter)* / Barbra Streisand *(Funny Girl)*
1969	John Wayne *(True Grit)*	Maggie Smith *(The Prime of Miss Jean Brodie)*
1970	George C. Scott (declined) *(Patton)*	Glenda Jackson *(Women in Love)*
1971	Gene Hackman *(The French Connection)*	Jane Fonda *(Klute)*
1972	Marlon Brando (declined) *(The Godfather)*	Liza Minnelli *(Cabaret)*
1973	Jack Lemmon *(Save the Tiger)*	Glenda Jackson *(A Touch of Class)*
1974	Art Carney *(Harry and Tonto)*	Ellen Burstyn *(Alice Doesn't Live Here Any More)*
1975	Jack Nicholson *(One Flew Over the Cuckoo's Nest)*	Louise Fletcher *(One Flew Over the Cuckoo's Nest)*
1976	Peter Finch (posthumous award) *(Network)*	Faye Dunaway *(Network)*
1977	Richard Dreyfuss *(The Goodbye Girl)*	Diane Keaton *(Annie Hall)*
1978	Jon Voight *(Coming Home)*	Jane Fonda *(Coming Home)*
1979	Dustin Hoffman *(Kramer vs. Kramer)*	Sally Field *(Norma Rae)*
1980	Robert De Niro *(Raging Bull)*	Sissy Spacek *(Coal Miner's Daughter)*

Advertising slogans from our youth: toiletries

- It's tingling fresh, it's fresh as ice, it's Gibbs SR toothpaste.
- You'll wonder where the yellow went when you brush your teeth with Pepsodent.
- Ultrabrite – a smile so bright it gets you noticed.
- Look, mum! No cavities! (Crest toothpaste).
- Brush away, the SR way!
- Sunny, silky, Sunsilk hair.
- Things happen after a Badedas bath.
- A little dab of Brylcreem on your hair gives you the Brylcreem bounce.
- Ask for Coty Fashion Matched lipstick – in the heavenly candy-striped case!
- When a man you've never met before suddenly gives you flowers (Impulse).
- Mum keeps you fresh (Mum deodorant).
- Quick, quick, quick, my Quickies! (Quickies tissues).
- For people who can't brush their teeth after every meal (Gleem toothpaste).
- Macleans white teeth mean healthy teeth, but half-clean teeth are not.
- The smile that wins is the Pepsodent smile!
- Pepsodent wins 3 to 1 over any other toothpaste!
- The toothpaste with hexachlorophene in the stripe (Signal).
- Soft, soft Scotties with wet strength.
- Soft, strong and very long (Andrex).
- There's a fragrance that's here to stay and they call it … "Charlie".
- Get the Colgate ring of confidence around you.
- B.O. Your best friend won't tell you (Lifebuoy soap).
- The soap of the stars! (Lux).
- The world's finest blade. (Wilkinson Sword).

Apollo astronauts

	Crew	Mission dates	Date of Moon Landing
Apollo 1	Virgil I "Gus" Grissom Edward H White II Roger B Chaffee	Died in capsule fire during launch pad test, January 27, 1967	
Apollo 7	Walter M Schirra Donn F Eisele R Walter Cunningham	October 11-22, 1968	
Apollo 8	Frank Borman Jim Lovell William Anders	December 21-27, 1968	
Apollo 9	James A McDivitt David R Scott Russell L Schweickart	March 3-13, 1969	
Apollo 10	Thomas P Stafford John W Young Eugene A Cernan	May 18-26, 1969	
Apollo 11	Neil Armstrong* Michael Collins Edwin "Buzz" Aldrin*	July 16-24, 1969	July 20, 1969
Apollo 12	Charles "Pete" Conrad* Dick Gordon Alan Bean*	November 14-24, 1969	November 19, 1969
Apollo 13	Jim Lovell Jack Swigert Fred Haise	April 11-17, 1970	
Apollo 14	Alan Shepard** Stuart Roosa Edgar Mitchell*	January 31-February 9, 1971	February 2, 1971
Apollo 15	David Scott* Al Worden James Irwin*	July 26-August 7, 1971	July 30, 1971
Apollo 16	John W Young* Ken Mattingly Charles Duke*	April 16-27, 1972	April 21, 1972
Apollo 17	Eugene Cernan* Ronald Evans Harrison Schmitt*	December 07-19, 1972	December 11, 1972

* Walked on Moon, ** Played golf on Moon

Countries that have joined the European Union by year

1957	Belgium, France, Italy, Luxembourg, The Netherlands, Germany.
1973	Denmark, Ireland, United Kingdom.
1981	Greece.
1986	Portugal, Spain.
1995	Austria, Finland, Sweden.
2004	Czech Republic, Estonia, Hungary, Latvia, Lithuania, Malta, Poland, Slovakia, Slovenia.
2007	Bulgaria, Romania.

Former currencies of countries that have adopted the Euro

Country	Former currency	Replaced by Euro as cash
Austria	Schilling	2002
Belgium	Belgian franc	2002
Cyprus	Cypriot pound	2008
Estonia	Kroon	2011
Finland	Markka	2002
France	Franc	2002
Germany	Mark	2002
Greece	Drachma	2002
Ireland	Pound	2002
Italy	Lira	2002
Luxembourg	Luxembourgian franc	2002
Malta	Maltese lira	2008
Monaco	Monegasque franc	2002
Netherlands	Guilder	2002
Portugal	Escudo	2002
San Marino	Sammarinese lira	2002
Slovakia	Koruna	2009
Slovenia	Tolar	2007
Spain	Peseta	2002
Vatican	Vatican lira	2002

World Cup winners

	Winner	Score	Runner-Up	Host nation
1950	Uruguay	2-1	Brazil	Brazil
1954	West Germany	3-2	Hungary	Switzerland
1958	Brazil	5-2	Sweden	Sweden
1962	Brazil	3-1	Czechoslovakia	Chile
1966	England	4-2	West Germany	England
1970	Brazil	4-1	Italy	Mexico
1974	West Germany	2-1	Netherlands	West Germany
1978	Argentina	3-1	Netherlands	Argentina
1982	Italy	3-1	West Germany	Spain
1986	Argentina	3-2	West Germany	Mexico
1990	West Germany	1-0	Argentina	Italy
1994	Brazil	3-2*	Italy	USA
1998	France	3-0	Brazil	France
2002	Brazil	2-0	Germany	Japan
2006	Italy	5-3*	France	Germany
2010	Spain	1-0	Netherlands	South Africa

* decided by penalty shoot-out

Changes in VAT rates

VAT was introduced in the UK on April 1, 1973 (seriously!).
The VAT rate for food, books and children's clothes is 0%;
otherwise the rates have changed as follows:

April 1973	Standard rate 10%
July 1974	Standard rate 8%
November 1974	Standard rate 8%; higher rate (used for petrol) 25%
April 1976	Standard rate 8%; higher rate 12.5%
June 1979	Single rate 15%
March 1991	Single rate 17.5%
April 1994	Standard rate 17.5%; reduced rate (used for domestic fuel) 8%; the aim was to increase this to 17.5% in April 1995.
September 1997	Standard rate 17.5%; reduced rate 5%
December 2008	Standard rate 15%; reduced rate 5%
January 2011	Standard rate 20%; reduced rate 5%

Pipesmokers of the Year

1964	Rupert Davies	1985	Jimmy Greaves
1965	Harold Wilson	1986	David Bryant
1966	Andrew Cruickshank	1987	Barry Norman
1967	Warren Mitchell	1988	Ian Botham
1968	Peter Cushing	1989	Jeremy Brett
1969	Jack Hargreaves	1990	Laurence Marks
1970	Eric Morecambe	1991	John Harvey-Jones
1971	Lord Shinwell	1992	Tony Benn
1973	Frank Muir	1993	Rod Hull
1974	Fred Trueman	1994	Ranulph Fiennes
1975	Campbell Adamson	1995	Jethro
1976	Harold Wilson	1996	Colin Davis
1977	Brian Barnes	1997	Malcolm Bradbury
1978	Magnus Magnusson	1998	Willie John McBride
1979	J B Priestley	1999	Trevor Baylis
1980	Edward Fox	2000	Joss Ackland
1981	James Galway	2001	Russ Abbot
1982	Dave Lee Travis	2002	Richard Dunhill
1983	Patrick Moore	2003	Stephen Fry
1984	Henry Cooper		

The award was discontinued after 2003 because of the ban on tobacco advertising.

Décor and accessories from your student days

Ashtrays made out of old vinyl records • bean bags • Che Guevara poster
cigarette rolling machine • guitar that you could barely play • headphones
incense burner • joss sticks • Kahlil Gibran's *The Prophet* paperback
Lord Of The Rings paperback • Mateus Rose wine bottle with candle in
it red lightbulbs • a sombrero from your travels

O-level exam questions

University of London General School Examination,
Monday, June 26, 1950: 2pm-4.30pm:

B (vii): Do you consider it desirable that boys should know how to cook and that girls should know how to use simple tools?

University of London Elementary Mathematics – 1: Arithmetic, Algebra and Numerical Trigonometry Ordinary Paper, *Tuesday, September 12, 1950: 2.30pm-5.30pm:*

1. The charges for electricity in a household were 15s a quarter and, in addition, ¾d for each unit used. In one quarter 808 units were used. If gas had been used, the quarterly charges would have been 2s 6d for meter rent and 1s 2d per therm consumed. Assuming 1 therm to be equivalent to 200 cu. ft., how many cubic feet of gas could have been consumed in the quarter if the total charges for gas had been the same as for electricity?

2. A 440yd running track consisted of two parallel straight parts, each 120yd long joined by semi-circular ends. Find the radius of a semi-circular end, correct to the nearest foot (take π to be 3.142). If a man runs round the track in 52.3 seconds, find his average speed in miles per hour, correct to three significant figures.

Joint Matriculation Board English Language, Ordinary,
Friday, June 13, 1952: 9.30am-12pm:

2. Write from **two** to **three** pages on **one** of the following:

(a) The pains and pleasures of growing up. (b) The attraction of Britain for visitors from abroad. (c) Hero worship. (d) Holiday camps. (e) Model railways. (f) The charm of birds. (g) "One must move with the times."

Joint Matriculation Board General Paper, Ordinary,
June 12, 1953: 2pm-5pm:

1. What differences are there between the powers and duties of the Queen, the Prime Minister and the President of the United States of America?

13. What precautions to maintain their health should be taken by a party of people living for some months **either** within the Arctic Circle **or** in a tropical jungle? Explain the reasons for these precautions.

20. Write a brief essay on the literature of **one** of the following: cricket, mountaineering, walking, travel, pet animals.

Joint Matriculation Board Mathematics (0 25) Syllabus B, Paper 1,
Thursday, June 13, 1968: 9.30am-12pm:

A 1 (a) Find the cost of a ton of butter bought wholesale at 2s 3d a lb.

B 11 (a) A car travels 170 miles from London to Exeter at an average speed of 30 miles per hour. Calculate the average speed over the whole journey.

Joint Matriculation Board Mathematics (0 25) Syllabus B, Paper 2,
Friday, June 14, 1968: 2pm-4.30pm:

A 1 (a) Find the total cost of 38 threepenny stamps, 48 fourpenny stamps and 95 sixpenny stamps.

Afterword

Phew! How was that for a rollercoaster ride through your addled memory?

Bet you'd forgotten half that stuff, hadn't you? And we equally bet that it brought back memories of some other things from your dim and distant past that even we'd forgotten.

That's the thing about the past; it's very personal. We all remember Elvis and the Suez crisis and Jubbly drinks, but one man's tin of Nescafé was another man's bottle of Camp coffee and chicory essence. One girl's "salt, mustard, vinegar, pepper" skipping rhyme was another girl's shopping list; and all those playground games were played slightly differently depending on whether you lived in Wigan or Winchester, Edinburgh or Eastbourne. The fear of the tawse was unknown to those south of Hadrian's wall, but there the cane loomed large instead.

So we hope that, school punishments apart, the memories were happy ones. We're sure they were because, you know what? We lived through the best times ever. The war was over, rock 'n' roll had just been invented, the Swingin' Sixties were on their way, along with Carnaby Street, Flower Power and all the rest of it. The days were always long and sunny, times were more innocent, we had freedom and fun, there was no political correctness, no 'elf "n" safety, not even any yellow lines on the roads. Ah, those were the days!

So next time some young flibbertigibbet calls you a grumpy old whatsit, just remind them that you've had a far better time than they can possibly imagine. Ding dong, carry on!